DAY BY DAY
WITH JESUS

Other Christopher Books in Print

DAY BY DAY WITH JESUS

Father John Catoir

Director, The Christophers

Stephanie Raha

Editor-in-Chief

Margaret O'Connell
Mary Riddle

Associate Editors

Alison Moran

Media Associate

THE CHRISTOPHERS, 12 East 48th Street, New York, NY 10017

ISBN # 0 - 939055 - 06 - 6

Scripture quotations in this publication are from the Revised Standard Version Bible, Catholic Edition, copyright © 1965 and 1966 by the Division of Christian Education of the National Council of Churches of Christ in the U.S.A. and the New Revised Standard Version Bible, Catholic Edition, copyright © 1989 by the Division of Christian Education of the National Council of the Churches of Christ in the United States of America and used by permission. Some additional quotes have been adapted for use.

Jesus said . . . All things have been handed over to Me by My Father; and no one knows the Son except the Father, and no one knows the Father except the Son and anyone to whom the Son chooses to reveal Him. Come to Me, all you that are weary and are carrying heavy burdens, and I will give you rest. Take My yoke upon you, and learn from Me; for I am gentle and humble in heart, and you will find rest for your souls. For My yoke is easy, and My burden is light.

Matthew 11:25,27-30

Introduction

This is the 50th Anniversary year of The Christophers, and I want to share with you the words that Father James Keller recorded in the preface of one of the earliest books.

"This book has been prepared for all those who desire to be Christophers — Christ-bearers; to assist them in the daily practice of reflection and prayer . . . It is meant for those who are anxious to take even one small step in reaching out with the love of Christ to all people.

"No matter how far removed from Christ one may be, he or she is never too far away to begin to be a Christ-bearer.

"Action springs out of reflection and prayer. The mind *sees*, and with the help that God supplies, the will is moved to *do*. Your every effort at prayer deepens and strengthens your own spiritual power. As your spiritual power deepens you will desire more and more to bring something of that power to others."

Father Keller always stressed the relationship between prayer and action as Jesus did, and that is the very reason for this book. It is our way of honoring the call to action Jesus Christ issued to His disciples: *Go forth to all the world . . . and teach them to observe all that I have commanded you.* Good example is the best way to teach anything of value.

Last year, in order to make Jesus Christ the centerpiece of this anniversary issue, I invited the readers of my weekly newspaper column to write to me about their personal relationships with the Lord. I explained my own feelings about Jesus, who is not only my Lord but my best friend. Jesus is my untrembling center. He is the Lamb of God who has truly atoned for the sins of all.

I experience His healing and forgiveness every morning as I begin each new day. Like the sunflower turning toward the sun, I turn to Him for warmth, comfort and wisdom.

Hundreds of people answered my invitation, and they expressed their deep love of Jesus so beautifully.

The sheer faith of these writers is wonderfully apparent; so too is God's constant desire to touch hearts. As St. Augustine said, "You would not have sought God had He not already been seeking you." God is unchanging love and we are the beloved children whom He seeks.

This book also contains a number of additional passages on prayer and spirituality which I hope will help you to grow closer to the Lord, day-by-day.

Before beginning your daily reading, pause long enough to remind yourself that you are in the presence of God. As Father Keller said: "No matter who you are or what you are, God is surrounding you right now with His loving care."

As you give thanks to the Lord for all His gifts, rest confidently in His love and be at peace.

Sincerely in Christ,

Father John Catoir

Lord, teach us to pray.
— Luke 11:1

The following thoughts on prayer are based on the writings of Abbot John Chapman (1862-1932). I offer them to you as we begin a new year.

■ The only way to pray well is to pray.

■ Begin where you find yourself. Do not force yourself into any feelings.

■ You can't get rid of the worries of this world or the questionings of the intellect, but you can give yourself to God.

■ Pure prayer is pure intention without words. Do not worry about what you *should* say. Just give yourself to God as best you can.

■ Distraction, dryness and desolation are normal. Jesus suffered temptation and desolation showing us that they are in fact part of being human.

■ Be with God, and simply be what God enables you to be at the moment.

■ If you bear some form of physical, emotional or mental suffering, do not get down on yourself. Suffering *is* often intolerable and it's okay to tell God that. Only trust that God will give you the necessary grace to bear it.

◀ ▶

January 2

May Christ dwell in your hearts through faith,
as you are being rooted and grounded in love.
I pray that you may have the power to
comprehend, with all the saints, what is the
breadth and length and height and depth, and
to know the love of Christ that surpasses
knowledge, so that you may be
filled with all the fullness of God.
— Ephesians 3:17-19

Every human being contains a divine spark within. Each of us can be a real and tangible expression of God's love in this world.

How we choose to express this love is a personal decision to be worked out in the privacy of one's conscience.

So take out a few minutes today and try to discern what God is asking of you.

Remember, the Kingdom of God is within you. Sometimes it's a gentle presence and sometimes it's a powerful passion for justice.

Listen for God's voice — and heed it.

◄ ►

The divine quality of love is hard to define in human terms.

St. John summed it up this way:

God is love, and those who abide in love
abide in God and God abides in them.
(1 John 4:16)

A child in California gave her own simple explanation when her mother asked her one day why she was so happy. The child said, "Because God loves me and I love Him."

Charles Morgan commented on the profound significance of eternal love: "There is no surprise more magical than the surprise of being loved. It is God's finger on man's shoulder."

Love is far more than sentiment or emotion. It is the force of Heaven itself sustaining us and enabling each of us to bring peace and joy to a fear-numbed world.

◀ ▶

God is faithful.
— *1 Corinthians 1:9*

"Jesus is my savior, redeemer and my provider. He died for my sins that I may be saved. He gave me life and faith.

"In this world where greed, pride, deceit and sin prevail, it isn't easy to do the will of Jesus Christ unless you have a deep relationship with God.

"When I took time to learn about Jesus my life changed. I read the Bible little by little and I try my very best to live by it in my own simple way. What is faith if it is not coupled with action?

"I try to follow the commandments of God. It is not too easy because it means serving others without thinking of being served; forgiving those who have hurt me and praying for them.

"Imagine me praying for those who have wronged me? Had you known me before you wouldn't believe it's me.

"I thank God for giving me life and a chance to change. I am not rich, but being close to the Lord makes me rich. I have found contentment."
— C.M., Pampanga, Philippines

◀ ▶

Lead me in your truth.
— *Psalm 25:5*

Our God is a gracious God. He wills that all of us *be saved and come to the knowledge of the truth.* (1 Timothy 2:4)

Some people come to the knowledge of the truth very early; some learn by trial and error; some only through the crucible of suffering. One thing, however, is universally true: God is unchanging love.

God offers Himself freely to everyone, equally. His light and strength are constantly and universally present in the world waiting to be discovered by us in the good example of our neighbors, in the noble thoughts we find in literature, and in homilies, in conversations and sometimes even in failure and mistakes.

Grace is God's self-gift to the world. It is not limited to isolated individuals. It is there in abundance for us all, always leaving us free. Those who do not cooperate with this bounty of Divine grace are probably spiritually blind, but God will heal their blindness if they but ask.

And as Blessed Julian of Norwich wrote, "all manner of things shall be well."

◄ ►

January 6

So faith, hope and love abide, these three: but
the greatest of these is love.
— 1 Corinthians 13:13

God's sheltering love is at the root of the Judeo-Christian heritage.

In every generation, holy men and woman have testified to God's love by their lives of dedication and service. But it isn't enough that we know about God's eternal love — each one of us is called upon to be a sign of it.

This is our greatest challenge: to communicate God's love to those around us, to become their refuge, their shelter in the storm of life.

Obviously, one person can't do all that needs to be done. But each one of us can do our job, and each one of us can carry out the responsibilities of our own life.

With trust in God and the desire to serve him, one person can accomplish great things.

◀ ▶

Never forget that you are important to God and to other people.

If repeated setbacks cause you to ask "What's the use?" take time for a prayerful reading of these words by John Henry Newman:

"God created me to do Him some definite service; He has committed some work to me which He has not committed to another. I have my mission. Therefore I will trust Him.

"Whatever, wherever I am, I can never be thrown away. If I am in sickness, my sickness may serve Him . . . if I am in sorrow, my sorrow may serve Him. He does nothing in vain. He knows what He is about."

Centuries ago, St. Paul stressed this same idea.

We do not live to ourselves and we do not die to ourselves. If we live, we live to the Lord, and if we die, we die to the Lord. Whether we live or whether we die, we are the Lord's.
(Romans 14:8)

◄ ►

By His wind the heavens were made fair.
— *Job 26:13*

"I came to know Jesus through my parents, grandparents, and the church, but most of all through His presence in confronting problems that sometimes arose. I just knew.

"I think of Jesus as a rugged man, perhaps not with the beautiful face that artists have portrayed over the years. He was a man of the times. He must have walked, talked, laughed, and cried and perhaps looked like so many of his Jewish peers.

"I often think if I were living during Christ's time, I would probably not have believed as so many didn't. But the one thing that keeps going through my mind as I read the Bible is that no other man could speak as He did. No other man could put things in such beautiful ways. There was no animosity or hatred. There was only kindness and compassion.

"My son at the age of four once asked me how I knew there was a Jesus. I did not hesitate but said, 'Do you feel the wind when it blows?' He said, 'Yes.' I said, 'But you cannot see the wind. Isn't this what Jesus is? He is always there but you cannot see Him. You just know.'"

— K.V., Houston, TX

◀ ▶

January 9

*Truly, I tell you, just as you did it to one of the
least of these who are members of My family,
you did it to Me.*
— *Matthew 25:40*

There are over 84 million volunteers in America
providing billions of dollars worth of free services
every year, giving away billions of work hours annually.

People volunteer for so many reasons: because
of their faith; to be needed; to help themselves
cope with loss or grief; to make new friends or
learn new skills.

Gladys Longo, a retired social worker and dia-
betic from Providence, RI, volunteered at local
chapters of the Lung Association and the American Diabetes Association. She also volunteered as
a court appointed advocate for neglected and
abused children.

In Philadelphia, 11-year-old Trevor Ferrell,
moved by the plight of the homeless, gave his own
pillow and extra blanket to a man sleeping on a
grate. Within a few years, he and his family had
opened a shelter for the homeless.

Whatever your gifts may be, you are needed.
Maybe you can find a couple of hours a month
to pursue some special interest as a volunteer.
Think about it.

◀ ▶

A glad heart makes a cheerful countenance, but
by sorrow of heart the spirit is broken.
— Proverbs 15:13

There isn't a day — or an hour — that goes
by when you aren't making some decision of one
kind or another. Some choices are fairly routine
and unremarkable, such as what to eat, what to
wear, what to watch on television. And then there
are important decisions regarding career, marriage,
education and so on.

But all of us have an especially profound power,
that of choosing our own attitude toward life and
its challenges. You can choose to hate, to hold
grudges, to despair, or you can decide to forgive,
to hold hope, to be grateful, to love, and to be
happy.

Such choices affect who you are and how you
relate to others and to God. God has planned an
eternity of happiness for you and He wants you
to enjoy His wonderful creation.

The greatest honor you can give to Almighty
God is to live gladly because of the knowledge
of His love.

January 11

A hopeful person sees an opportunity in every calamity, while a cynic sees a calamity in every opportunity.

One unknown author put it this way: "A pessimist is one who feels bad when he feels good for fear he'll feel worse when he feels better."

Accustom yourself to think hopefully under the most disheartening circumstances and you will be able to say with the Hebrew Psalmist:

Happy are those whose help is the God of Jacob, whose hope is in the Lord, their God, Who made heaven and earth, the sea and all that is in them; Who keeps faith forever.
(Psalm 146:5-6)

◀ ▶

I trust in You, O Lord, I say, "You are my God."
— Psalm 31:14

"I have never in my life wavered in my love for the Lord. This doesn't, however, mean that I have never questioned Him. I have. But it isn't because I don't trust in Him. It's simply because I don't understand human suffering.

"I've had my share of crosses to carry, in my fifty-six years of life, but I swear, I wouldn't trade one of them, because in all of my troubled days, I always knew where to go. I would go straight to God. I can't remember one time when He hasn't answered me. I don't mean He answers me in the way I tell Him to but He does it in the way that's best for me.

"He is my ultimate love. He's the only one in this world that I can always count on because He's always there."

— R.H. Salt Lake City, UT

◀ ▶

Some people have a way of being their own worst enemy. Constant self-criticism has been called the tyranny of the super-ego. The demon within can be a slave driver: "I must do this; I must do that; I must stop this or that . . ."

But God's supreme law calls us to love ourselves, and to be kind to ourselves. As we cling to God, it is all a matter of trust.

Blessed are those who trust in the Lord . . .
They shall be like trees planted by water, sending
out their roots by the stream. They shall not fear
when heat comes, and their leaves shall stay green;
in the year of drought they are not anxious,
and they do not cease to bear fruit.
(Jeremiah 17:7-8)

We begin to trust by looking first to God rather than others. Because Jesus abides in us through grace, our Father in heaven looks on us with favor:

You are My Child, the Beloved; with You
I am well pleased. (Luke 3:22)

And when we are thrown back on ourselves by problems and sorrows, we turn confidently to the One within for whom we were made, and the One who desires intimacy with us.

The spiritual life is nothing more than our intimate relationship with God.

◀ ▶

January 14

*Let your speech always be gracious,
seasoned with salt, so that you may know how
you ought to answer everyone.*
— *Colossians 4:6*

A best seller, a song, an office memo, a note that says, "I love you." They all start with words on a blank sheet of paper, or in today's world, a blank computer screen.

Consider for a moment the great power of words. The words you speak, the words you read, the words you write . . . words of inspiration, courage and love. They call forth the best that is in you.

Your words on a note or a phone message can light a spark of hope in someone who needs what only you can give.

The right words — your words — can make a difference for your loved ones, your community, your world.

◄ ►

Those who do not love a brother or sister
whom they have seen, cannot love God
whom they have not seen.
— 1 John 4:20

Father
You have made us all.
Red, yellow, brown, white and black
tall and short, fat and thin
rich and poor, young and old —
all are Your children.
Teach us to cooperate rather than to compete
to respect rather than to revile
to forgive rather than condemn.
Your Son turned away from no one.
May we learn, like Him, to be open to others,
to the share of the divine
that You have implanted
in each of Your sons and daughters.
And may we forge a bond of love
that will make a living reality
the brotherhood in which we profess to believe.
Amen.

◀ ▶

With Him I speak face to face —
clearly, not in riddles.
— Numbers 12:8

"Jesus to me is first and foremost my friend. He takes on, therefore, all the qualities I look for in a friend. He is loving, kind, challenging, always wanting the best for me. He is someone I'm most comfortable with. I don't feel uncomfortable if I can't find words to say to Him. I just enjoy His silent presence.

"Our relationship is not a bed of roses. There are times when I get angry with Him. There are times I can't understand Him.

"Most of the time we are happy together. We make a great team when there are things to be done. I am constantly aware of His presence and in any decisions I always invoke Him in one way or another.

"We dream together about how we can make the world a better place. He is the center of my life. I don't publicly say it in so many words, but I hope that by my life, people can get to know Him.

"He is also someone I have fallen deeply in love with — lover, brother, friend — all in one."

— Y.V., Port Elizabeth, South Africa

◀ ▶

Jesus told us about the nature of God by what He did and said. Remember when Philip said,

"Lord, show us the Father, and we shall be satisfied." Jesus replied, "Have I been with you all this time, Philip, and you do not know Me? Whoever has seen Me has seen the Father . . . I am in the Father and the Father is in Me."
(John 14:8-9,11)

Think for a moment about the public ministry of Jesus. He was continually reaching out to the poor, the dispossessed, the outcasts, the lepers.

Jesus rebuked the rash judgment of those who condemned the woman taken in adultery. He forgave sinners.

Every word, every gesture of Jesus, right up to His suffering and death, showed us that God reaches out to those in need. We learn that God is a loving, caring Father. This wonderful truth may be impossible to appreciate fully, but it is true nonetheless.

◄ ►

> *No eye has seen, nor ear heard, nor the*
> *human heart conceived, what God has*
> *prepared for those who love Him.*
> — *1 Corinthians 2:9*

These majestic words of the apostle Paul are not only intended as a description of heaven, they also describe the fullness of life that we can experience here on earth when our lives are lived in the Lord.

Faith in God doesn't eliminate all of our earthly problems, but faith does give us the vision to see ourselves and our problems in a truer light.

If you open your heart to Him, you'll discover God is already within you, waiting to share His strength and His joy. He asks only one thing in return, your love.

Remember, true love is in the will — the will to give yourself to God.

◀ ▶

In Him we live and move and have our being.
— *Acts 17:28*

A noted doctor surprised a friend by pausing to say a brief prayer before a difficult operation.

"I thought a surgeon relied solely on his ability," his visitor remarked.

"A surgeon is only human," he replied. "He cannot work miracles by himself. I am certain science could not have advanced as far as it has were it not for something far greater and stronger than mere man."

Then he explained, "I feel so close to God when I am operating that I don't know where my skill leaves off and His begins."

The more you realize you are in the Divine Presence at all times, the more likely you are to turn to the Lord for guidance and strength.

Give your best to the task before you, and always begin with a prayer.

◄ ►

He went down with them and came to Nazareth,
and was obedient to them; and His mother
kept all these things in her heart.
— Luke 2:51

"When I was eleven years old, my parents enrolled me in a parochial school. On the back wall of the classroom was a picture of the Holy Family. Jesus was depicted as a child of my own age and since His earthly guardian was Joseph — same name as my father — I felt immediately friendly toward Jesus. Later I learned that the Holy Family was poor, just like my parents who worked hard and honestly.

"I wondered about Jesus. In His early manhood, He must have helped Joseph. Did they transport the furniture they made to their customers? Did they build houses and barns?

"I imagined Mary as an intelligent, industrious homemaker, just like Mom who washed, ironed, sewed, kept roomers, prepared delicious meals. She had a lively disposition and sang little songs, albeit out of tune.

"Paradoxically, to the worldly wise, our all-powerful Lord Jesus was a model for human humility. His example gives me a certain poise, a tendency not to be impressed by the rich and successful people in our society."

— M.F., Newton, MA

◀ ▶

January 21

*Is there anyone among you who, if your child
asks for a fish, will give a snake instead of
a fish? Or if the child asks for an egg,
will give a scorpion?*
— Luke 11:11-13

Being a young man or woman these days
doesn't necessarily mean being carefree. Young
people have serious pressures on them: the drug
and alcohol subculture, fear of unemployment
and peer pressure.

They need to ventilate. They need someone who
will take the time to listen. Listening can be the
greatest gift you can give a young person. Make
time to listen to the trivial events in their lives;
eventually the big things will surface.

Parents who fail to listen say things like, "I can't
be bothered, I'm busy." In effect they are saying,
"You're not important to me." The teen hears that
message loud and clear.

If teens are important to you and if you're worried about the problems they face, learn to become
a skilled listener. It will pay big dividends in the
years ahead.

◄ ►

*Whoever speaks must do so as one
speaking the very words of God; whoever
serves must do so with the strength that God
supplies, so that God may be glorified in
all things through Jesus Christ.*
— 1 Peter 4:11

We honor God when we use our talents to enhance the lives of others.

We honor God when we enjoy the wonders of His creation, the beauty of nature, the laughter of children.

We honor God when we live joyfully, because of the knowledge of His love.

Religion is not meant to be a gloom and doom enterprise. It begins with God's love for us. It is nourished by our love for one another and it is fully realized in our love for God.

◀ ▶

January 23

*The heavens are telling the glory of God,
and the firmament proclaims
His handiwork.
— Psalm 19:1*

The glory of the universe — from the smallest blade of grass to the planets and stars millions of miles away — all testify to the wondrous design of a loving Creator.

Sublime as it is, the beauty and order of the heavens cannot compare with the splendor of His greatest handiwork, the human race.

When we use our liberty to make His divine love the basis of all our actions, we are true replicas of our Maker.

Show proper respect for the divine image that is reflected in you and in every person, without exception.

◄ ►

> *Believe in the Lord Jesus
> and you will be saved.*
> — *Acts 16:31*

"Jesus Christ was once a man and understands how I feel. Jesus is God, and there is nothing He does not understand.

"Jesus is the person who lovingly welcomed me when I left Him for awhile when I pursued a sinful life. He has seen all my sorrows, joys, accomplishments and failures. He helps explain me to myself. He helps me understand others. Jesus Christ, my God, desires always to help me and He wants to help everyone who asks.

"Jesus sent me the Holy Spirit to help me. It began at my Baptism and has been increased by receiving Jesus in the sacrament of Holy Eucharist. I have been lovingly forgiven and grace has been restored to me when I confessed my sins in the sacrament of Reconciliation. Jesus is always there, patiently waiting for me to come to Him in the sacraments and prayer.

"Jesus Christ shows me His goodness through His forgiveness and intense love. He blesses me with all the important things I need for my life on earth and in life everlasting."

— M.M., Boca Raton, FL

◄ ►

*Come away by yourselves
to a lonely place,
and rest a while.*
— *Mark 6:31*

Is it really necessary to always go to a desert to pray?

I don't think so. Carlo Carretto, who left Italy for the desert to pray, said that "to pray is to love." In his book, *In Search of the Beyond*, he wrote, "Prayer transcends space and can be lived anywhere, since wherever you love, Love is there, for God is love."

To pray is to love. Pure prayer is in the will to cling to God in all circumstances and to become an instrument of His love.

"Love is the highest form of prayer — it is the fullness of prayer," says Carretto.

And if prayer is love, you don't have to go to the desert to pray. It happens whenever the love of God flows through you.

◀ ▶

Most people have had the experience of getting to the end of a television program with only a vague awareness of what it was all about. Sometimes, that experience happens to us when it comes to religion. We're not really paying attention. We're not really involved.

Christians believe that God is love. But many of them have no experience of His love as a real comfort in their lives.

It's not enough just to know that God loves you. You have to experience that love by claiming it.

Jesus said, *These things I have spoken to you, that My joy may be in you, and that your joy may be full.* (John 15:11)

Ponder these words. As you do, you'll become more and more aware that God loves you with an infinite love. And as you do become more aware of this great mystery, you'll be better able to live gladly because of the knowledge, the personal experience of His love.

> *Be still*
> *and know that I am God.*
> *— Psalm 46:10*

Everyone needs a quiet time to sit down and think — to contemplate. The word contemplation itself means to consider thoughtfully, to meditate upon.

Contemplation is a form of prayer.

The French philosopher Descartes said: "In order to improve the mind, we ought less to learn, than to contemplate."

By whatever name you may choose to call it, reflect occasionally on the deeper meaning of life; raise your heart to Him who placed you in this world for a definite purpose.

Contemplation is not incompatible with action. In fact it leads to positive action. It helps ensure that whatever we do in life will be based on sound judgment and high motivation.

To contemplate is to absorb God's love in silence.

◄ ►

> *In this place I will give you prosperity,*
> *says the Lord of hosts.*
> *— Haggai 2:9*

"I begin my day with an attitude of joy and thanksgiving. I am happy to be so grateful and have peace of mind. Jesus helps me pray for others and blesses me with love and consideration for my family and friends.

"I trust in Jesus Christ. I thank Him for the freedom to follow my inner guidance. He is my comfort. When I get confused, frustrated and question how am I going to do all I want to do, I let go by giving up the negative. I let God take over, by turning within for order, peace and light. I build up my spiritual awareness. I believe firmly that the Lord has guided me to unscramble my schedule and set my priorities.

"The deeper your faith, the closer you feel to Jesus Christ and the greater your ability to have good thoughts! I pray in silence and aloud. I pray in song, with words and without. I pray with people and alone.

"I always thank our Lord for the prosperity he gives — joy and blessings."

— S.A., Toms River, NJ

◄ ►

Ask for the ancient paths,
where the good way is;
and walk in it.
— Jeremiah 6:16

Think for a moment about the power of love. It's the only thing in the world that holds everything together. I think of it as a spiritual force, holding all the world's atoms in perfect proportion.

It isn't so much what you do in life; it's what you allow God to do through you. If you are open to the Spirit of Love, God will lead you away from self-preoccupation. "He will lead you along paths you would not have chosen for yourself" as Evelyn Underhill wrote.

Love is not always easy or pleasureful because often it is bound up with the cross. But true love can make the crosses of life easy to carry.

Resolve to grow closer to God by expanding your love. Today let your work, and your leisure time, include many acts of loving kindness.

◄ ►

*Night and day we pray most earnestly
that we may see you face to face and restore
whatever is lacking in your faith.*
— *1 Thessalonians 3:10*

Every day, all around the world, millions of people from various faith traditions pause to pray.

They find solace in private devotion and community worship. Prayer is turning one's mind and heart to an all-loving God. It is trusting in His mercy and support. Formal words are useful, but sometimes they're not necessary.

Prayer begins in the heart, but true prayer is in the will, the will to give yourself to God.

Prayer, above all, is stopping everything else you're doing long enough to place yourself in God's presence.

So, lift up your heart and have a new confidence in the love of God. The Lord is closer to you than your own heartbeat.

◄ ►

January 31

So teach us to number our days that we may get a heart of wisdom.
— Psalm 90:12

The following is a prayer for those growing old. But it offers something to think about — whatever your age.

Father,
Help me to accept the lessening of my powers with realism and good humor.

Keep me from self-pity, and remind me that age has not taken away my mission in life, but only altered it.

Grant me a taste for the hidden beauty of creation, a continuing interest in Your world — and mine.

Make me more patient with myself, more tolerant of the foibles of others, more outgoing with the timid and shy.

Bestow on me a greater readiness for prayer, and a humble acceptance of suffering.

Deepen my faith in Your unfailing truth. Strengthen my hope so I can better share in the joy of Your Son's resurrection.

Increase my love for the Holy Spirit — with whom I am destined to share my life for all eternity.

Amen.

◄ ►

February 1

Love one another as I have loved you.
— John 15:12

"In this human life we live, there can be no greater joy — no greater consolation — no greater strength than to know that I am loved by God, totally.

"Jesus' life has shown me something of that love. I see the continual compassion He had for the multitudes. I see the great deeds of kindness, to the point of miracles, that He did to ease sufferings and sorrows.

"In my daily life, He is always there for me. In the rough times there were great opportunities to grow in virtues I did not have. And most striking of all, in those trials, there came unexpected help, greater than I could possibly have imagined or expected, and from the most unlikely sources. At other times too that help was an insight, a slowly surging strength that rose up from somewhere within.

"And I knew — it came from Jesus, who truly loves me!"

— M.F., Sydney, Nova Scotia

◄ ►

February 2

And the peace of God,
which passes all understanding,
will keep your hearts and your minds
in Christ Jesus.
— Philippians 4:7

In her book, "Guest of the Revolution," Kathryn Koob tells how daily periods of prayer and meditation sustained her during her 444 days as a hostage in Iran.

At first, she had only a hymnal and the Scripture verses she had memorized as a child to aid her in prayer. Later she was given a Bible. Of herself and her roommate, another woman hostage, Miss Koob says, "Our strength came to be the trust we had that God would somehow use us, take care of us, and provide for us."

In talks given after the ordeal, she said, "To seek the Lord in our aloneness is to gain a special measure of His strength and His wisdom, and the peace that passeth all understanding."

◄ ►

February 3

Before I formed you in the womb,
I knew you,
and before you were born
I consecrated you.
— *Jeremiah 1:5*

All human life is sacred.

Our reverence for life urges us to seek new and better ways to:

■ remove unjust social conditions
■ to reduce the levels of poverty and ignorance
■ to raise the quality of life on all levels.

Human life is sacred from the first moment of conception to the final moment of death. The right to be born is a divine right.

Compassionate care for the unwed mother who needs our help is part of our reverence for life.

Our standards and beliefs are set down in Holy Scripture.

◄ ►

February 4

> *Speak, Lord,*
> *for Your servant is listening.*
> — *Samuel 3:9*

What makes a person special?

I think it's his or her capacity to love. And the capacity to love is enhanced by the ability to listen.

Train yourself to listen. Listening is a gift — a priceless gift for you to give to others.

Offer this little prayer today, to help yourself become a better listener:

Teach me to be still, Lord
That I may truly hear my brothers and sisters.
Teach me to listen more attentively, as a way of
expressing my love. And teach me to
understand that it is through their voices
That I will come to know Yours.

Amen.

◄ ►

February 5

(Jesus) was praying in a certain place,
and when He ceased,
one of His disciples said to Him,
"Lord, teach us to pray."
— Luke 11:1

Teach us to pray.

Jesus responded to His disciples' request by teaching them the prayer we call the "Our Father" or the "Lord's Prayer."

It's a perfect prayer. Whenever you're in emotional pain, say it slowly over and over again.

The Lord Himself taught us the words. In this prayer we reverence God, we release ourselves from the past through forgiveness, and we trust the future to God's loving care and protection.

Believe that God really loves you and live this day as a joyful child of God.

◀ ▶

February 6

He will feed His flock like a shepherd.
— Isaiah 40:11

"I had turned from God for a period in my life. However, Jesus called to me, I heard Him and opened myself to Him. He forgave me and welcomed me back to His fold. In everything I do or think now, Jesus takes a part. I can't read or hear enough about Him.

"Why did it take me so long? I have always believed in Jesus, but suddenly a truth hits you in a new way. It all makes sense now. In His own time God makes Himself known to us. I suppose He has called me a thousand times, but I just didn't answer Him. How grateful I am that He was so persistent.

"I used to be a fearful person. Miss Anxious, Miss Worrywart, that was me. I was anxious over everything and everybody.

"Now, I try to give myself to God each morning and walk away. How wonderful to have that sack taken from my shoulders by my friend, Jesus. He carries my burden so that I can stand up straight."
— M.K., Bayonne, NJ

◀ ▶

February 7

Everyone has those days when everything seems to go wrong. Days when we feel abandoned — by everybody — even by God.

Jesus understood that feeling well. He was in touch with men and women under stress all of His life. On every side He saw crowds of people feeling dejected and helpless. They didn't know where to turn.

To give them hope, He reminded them of the countless birds of the air, not one of them unknown to our Heavenly Father.

He assured His followers that there is no need to be afraid. That each and every person is valuable in the sight of God.

Take comfort in Christ's compassionate words:

Look at the birds of the air — they neither sow nor reap nor gather in barns, and yet your Heavenly Father feeds them. Are you not of more value than they? (Matthew 6:26)

If God cares so much for these small creatures, His love for you is beyond question.

◄ ►

February 8

*The whole law is summed up in a
single commandment, "You shall
love your neighbor as yourself."*
— *Galatians 5:14*

A dying miner, trapped in a West Virginia coal mine, scribbled these final words to his wife: "I love you more than you will ever know. Take care of the kids and raise them to serve the Lord."

When rescue workers finally reached the dead man, eight days later, they found the note attached to his safety lamp.

The brief message, written in a dark underground death chamber, is an eloquent tribute to the dead miner. To have expressed such devotion to his family and his God, despite the harrowing circumstances, meant that his heart and soul had long been trained in a divinely rooted love.

Whether your life is long or short, be sure to learn the only lesson that counts for all eternity — to love God above all else and your neighbor as yourself.

◀ ▶

*Render true judgments, show kindness and
mercy to one another; do not oppress the
widow, the orphan, the alien, or the poor;
and do not devise evil in your hearts
against one another.*
— *Zechariah 7:9-10*

Is the virtue of kindness a trait cultivated by
good breeding? Is it merely politeness, civility,
graciousness? Or is it more?

Obviously there is a counterfeit kindness that
has little to do with the supernatural virtue of
charity. Kidnappers are kind to their victims.
Sycophants are kind to their superiors. Seducers
use kindness to get what they want.

But true kindness is a supernatural virtue. It
produces a sweetness that transcends the natural
order. It is informed by the strength of the risen
Christ. Under its influence people are motivated
to be charitable in all circumstances: to turn the
other cheek; to return good for evil; to bless those
who persecute them and to forgive seventy times
seven.

Show kindness today in all that you do.

◄ ►

> *(God) said,*
> *"Let light shine in the darkness."*
> *— 2 Corinthians 4:6*

For nearly half a century, The Christophers have been challenging individuals around the world to become carriers of divine love and divine truth. Three essential beliefs inspire the Christopher message:

First, the belief that everyone has a God-given mission. Second, the conviction that one person, namely you, can make a difference. And finally, the realization that the most effective way to make a difference is through positive, constructive action.

When these three beliefs are combined, the tremendous power and potential of any individual can be utilized to make this a better world. Start by asking yourself, "What can I do?"

*You shall not take vengeance
or bear a grudge
against any of your people,
but you shall love your neighbor
as yourself.*
— *Leviticus 19:18*

"What I believe about Jesus Christ is an evolving, dynamic thing. When Jesus tells us to love our neighbor and even our enemy, I believe He's telling us not to cut anyone off just because they don't call this Creator by the same name as we do.

"Jesus is the human connection — wholly human and wholly the Great Power, God. This Creator whose children call him by different names, calls me by my own name and tells me to stop sweating the small stuff and start reaching out with love and healing to every person with whom I come in contact, from the cashier in the supermarket, to my own immediate family, to the Pope in Rome, or the Queen in England.

"So to me Jesus is the one who shows us how to love and to accept each other, here, now, today, in this place where we are."

— P.M., Wyckoff, NJ

◄ ►

One day you will have the consolation of saying with St. Paul:

I have fought the good fight,
I have finished the race, I have kept the faith.
(2 Timothy 4:7)

When you accept a position of responsibility, don't be surprised by the troubles, problems, disappointments and misunderstandings that go with it. One man called such trials "penalties of leadership."

Far from being disheartened by the hardships of leadership or parenthood, regard them as a badge of honor. It is usually the best possible proof that you are on the right track.

Our Lord, the Leader of leaders, constantly reminds all who would be effective Christ-bearers that they must earn their battle scars. He said frankly:

If they have persecuted Me,
they will persecute you.
(John 15:20)

Look beyond the heartaches and heartbreaks that you are bound to encounter. They are the lot of every worthwhile leader. Never forget that you are winning most while you seem to lose.

◄ ►

My heart recoils within Me,
My compassion grows warm and tender.
— Hosea 11:8

It's worth remembering that God loves us not because we are good, but because we are little.

He wants us to be good, but our success or failure does not change His attitude toward us. God's love is constant and unchanging.

God loves us and allows us to remain prone to sin to teach us the importance of depending on Him. If God loved only those who were not sinners, there would be no one at all for Him to love.

Being a true lover, God doesn't smother or overpower the beloved. He treats each loved one with respect, giving him or her the freedom to respond without duress.

God leads us ever so gently to heaven, where there are no love-slaves, but only lovers who are fully free, fully alive.

◄ ►

Let love be genuine;
hate what is evil,
hold fast to what is good;
love one another with affection.
— Romans 12:9,10

The world around us often seems to be a world without love — a world where so many people appear to be unable to respect and love themselves and one another.

This isn't the world that God wants for us.

In His divine plan, love is the key ingredient. And every individual is called to use his or her God-given talents to the fullest potential.

No matter what your limitations might be, your unique blend of gifts, experiences, insights and talents are needed in this world. And when you accept and build upon your personal gifts, the whole world benefits.

Life becomes far richer because of the love and beauty that only you can bring to it.

◀ ▶

February 15

Where the Spirit of the Lord is,
there is freedom.
— *2 Corinthians 3:17*

"Jesus is my best friend, the one friend I can depend on, day in and day out, to always be ready to listen to me, to lend a sympathetic ear, to overlook my faults (large and small), and to let me know that He is always near.

"Each night at prayer, I try to thank Him for the great gifts He has given to me. By dying on the cross for me He gave me life. And, as if that wasn't enough, He sent me His Holy Spirit, the ultimate gift of Love.

"He is the Rock of my existence. When I face a crisis I can face it because I know that He is anchoring me in strength and certainty, shouldering the entire load and making it possible for me to remain at peace. This peace is then transmitted to others who take their strength from this peace.

"He said that our lives are to be our witness, so that others may see that His peace is truly the peace which surpasses all understanding.

"I can't imagine why He loves me so. All I can say is, 'Thank you, Jesus, for everything.' "
— C.M., Millburn, NJ

◀ ▶

> *Blessed are the pure of heart,*
> *for they will see God.*
> — *Matthew 5:8*

Look up on a clear night and what do you see? A random scattering of stars?

It may seem that way, but navigators can pick out patterns that enable them to steer a ship safely home.

Look at an X-ray and what do you see? Light and shadow, yes; but a technician can identify the tiniest fracture of a bone.

We see what we're trained to see. And much depends on what we're looking for.

The *pure of heart* look for the good in others.

And when they see the good in others, they are catching a glimpse of God Himself.

◄ ►

*Little children, let us not love in word or
speech but in deed and in truth.*
— *1 John 3:18*

Jesus said He wanted us to prove that we are
His disciples by the way we love one another. I
came across a commentary on the Gospel of John
by St. Jerome which sheds some interesting light
on how the early church resonated with this
insight.

"In his old age at Ephesus, Blessed John the
Evangelist could barely be supported into Church
on the arms of his disciples, nor could he say more
than a few words when he got there. At each service he would only repeat: 'My little children, love
one another.'

"Finally, the disciples and brothers and sisters
who were wearied by such constant repetition, said
to him, 'Master, why do you always say the same
thing?' The reply was simple, 'Because it is the
Lord's command, and if you do only this, it suf-
fices.'"

Jesus didn't ask us to have warm feelings for
one another. He asked for love and that implies
the will to cleanse oneself of selfishness.

Today try to improve the way you love others
so as to be more pleasing to the Lord.

◀ ▶

Above all hold unfailing your love for one another, since love covers a multitude of sins. Practice hospitality ungrudgingly to one another. As each one has received a gift, employ it for one another, as good stewards of God's varied grace.
— *1 Peter 4:8-10*

The work of understanding and explaining our faith is a job for every believer. It's not just a job for professional theologians or publishers. Whether it's with parents or teachers or friends or fellow workers, all of us are called upon to witness to our faith in our lives.

Sometimes this witness is better made in deeds rather than words, in acts of kindness and generosity. The most effective testimony you can give to your faith is to become an instrument of God's love and God's peace.

Look for those opportunities to deepen your commitment to the gospel ideals of love and service for the benefit of those around you.

February 19

And God said, "Ask what I should give you."
— 1 Kings 3:5

"My personal relationship with the Lord is very strong today because of my mother. Four years ago, my mother walked in the door and said, 'I have breast cancer.'

"Well, I cried very hard for two days straight. I got down on my knees to pray to the Lord, 'I need more time with my mother.' Mom was supposed to have tests done the next day to see if it had gone to the bones. The call came from my father, 'There's no cancer in her bones.' We rejoiced.

"Four years passed. Mom kept her battle with cancer strong. We did everything in our power to help her emotionally and physically.

"Three months ago, the doctor found tumors in her liver and bones. Mom and I both knew it would come to this. She was not ready to go but became more accepting as days went by.

"I asked the Lord, 'If you must take my mom, please take her gently.' The Lord heard my prayers. He took her to a really beautiful place. She went ever so gently."

— B.Z., Bronson, IA

◄ ►

February 20

*The greatest among you must become like the
youngest, and the leader like the
one who serves.*
— Luke 22:26

We can be leaders without formal titles or positions. The following prayer is for all of us.

Jesus, You said that anyone who wants to be a leader must learn to be everyone's servant. At times I find that hard to accept.

Teach me why You became everyone's servant.

Teach me why the truly great leaders — those who accomplished the greatest good for the largest number of people — were men and women who knew that to lead is to serve.

Motivate me to begin leading those I meet daily by discovering their needs and striving to help them live up to their potential.

Amen

February 21

God so loved the world that He gave
His only Son that whoever believes in Him
should not perish but have eternal life.
For God sent the Son into the world not
to condemn the world, but that the world
might be saved through Him.
(John 3:16-17)

It takes courage to reach out as Jesus did.

It takes courage to love others well: in caring for children, in witnessing to our faith, in being an example for others, in working conscientiously at our job, in being kind to our neighbors, in all the tasks of daily life. All this takes courage.

Participation in the corporate destiny of humankind calls for a love of justice, too. So much pain and injustice exists all around us.

We need to see the world as Jesus sees it.

He fought against the evils that create untold suffering in the human family and He wants us to do the same.

> *Blessed are the peacemakers,*
> *for they shall be called children of God.*
> *— Matthew 5:9*

Here's a prayer in support of The Christophers'
belief that there's nobody like you, and you can
make a difference:

Father,
Grant that I may be a bearer of Christ
Jesus, Your Son.
Strengthen me, by Your Spirit, to change
the world around me for the better.
Nourish in me a practical desire to build up
rather than tear down.
Make me more energetic in seeking
solutions to the problems that confront all
of us.
Never let me forget that it is better to light
one candle than to curse the darkness.
Father, sustain me in the hope that, one
day, I may join my light with Yours.

Amen.

The Lord is near to the brokenhearted, and
saves the crushed in spirit.
— Psalm 34:18

"In 1983 I was the head of a trading desk at a firm on Wall Street. All was going so well until darkness entered my life.

"I lost my health, my well-being and was betrayed. It was indeed a very dark time. No matter how hard I fought I just could not get back on my feet. I told people how I felt but no one could really understand. I was looking for a friend, a good friend.

"One day I picked up the Bible and really read it for the first time. I remember saying to myself, 'Jesus understands, He suffered the Passion.' Once I turned to Him things slowly started to improve. He also gave me something I did not ask for, faith. He treated me like a kid in a candy store.

"I wanted to return the love He showed me. So I left my job on Wall Street in 1984 to start a foundation. Since that time we have helped over 3,000 children with serious illnesses.

"As I look back I realize I had to be broken myself to understand the suffering of another. I was blind and He made me see."

— T.K., New Monmouth, NJ

◀ ▶

Humankind was created out of the dust.
In the fullness of His knowledge
the Lord distinguished them and
appointed their different ways.
— *Sirach 33:10,11*

Each musician enriches an orchestra by the individual touch he or she brings.

This was confirmed by an audio engineer who explained: "Violinists must play very closely together to produce good music, but far enough apart, in pitch and timing, to achieve a richness, an aliveness, which they would not have if they were playing precisely alike."

If each violinist in the orchestra played exactly the same way, the effect would sound like the amplification of a single instrument.

The "personal touch" you add to life cannot be duplicated by any other person in the world.

You have been entrusted by the Lord with talent of your own. Through it you can add your own particular contribution of love and beauty to a world much in need of it.

◄ ►

*From one ancestor (God) made all
the nations to inhabit the whole earth ... so
that they would search for God and perhaps
grope for Him and find Him — though indeed
He is not far from each one of us. For "In
Him we live and move and have our being."*
— Acts 17:26, 27-28

God is as close to you as your own soul.

He dwells in the intimate depth of your being.
Your unique personality grows out of His Being
and is rooted in God's own creative imagination.

Just as a great work of art emerges from the
mind of the artist, so do you spring forth from
God's mind.

The original idea of you is still in His mind.
Though now you are free to move away from that
idea if you choose.

Finding God's plan for you in life is finding
your true identity.

◀ ▶

> *Be imitators of God, as beloved children,*
> *and live in love, as Christ loved us.*
> — *Ephesians 5:1-2*

Love flows from person to person or it doesn't flow at all. That's what good family communication is all about.

When there is openness and honesty between husband and wife, parent and child, brother and sister, there is a comfortable atmosphere in the home.

Creating this atmosphere of emotional comfort is the responsibility of each family member.

The most important thing family members have to communicate is that they love each other.

When we love, we build trust and mutual respect. When we love, we become whole as individuals and as a family. When we love one another, we build a happy community.

◀ ▶

> *I know your works, your toil*
> *and your patient endurance.*
> — *Revelation 2:2*

"Jesus is someone I can talk to and turn to at any time, day or night, at home or at work.

"Having worked in the restaurant business for the past twenty years, I know firsthand how it is to deal with demanding customers. When I come close to losing it, I immediately turn to Jesus and ask Him to give me His strength and patience to deal with this circumstance.

"Oftentimes I meditate on the Carrying of the Cross, and think of how I can offer up my frustrations to God as a sacrifice, and in return He gives me the patience I earnestly desire and need. When things don't go my way, I think of how St. Francis taught us to offer up difficulties and humiliations as a sacrifice to God, and how to receive spiritual joy out of this.

"I often picture Jesus standing next to me with His arms outstretched ready to embrace me and engulf me in His love and tenderness. This thought alone can usually help me overcome any difficulties."

— N.W., Gaithersburg, MD

◀ ▶

Loose the bonds of injustice . . . share your
bread with the hungry . . . Then your light
shall break forth like the dawn, and your
healing shall spring up quickly.
— *Isaiah 58:6,7,8*

Deep within each person there is a restless search for harmony.

It is here that God touches our being, whether He is recognized or not.

Despite the apathy, cynicism, despair or rebellion all around us, many people want to know, "What can I do?" Theirs is an expression of hope and a plea for guidance.

This double search — for inner peace and outward direction — is sure to end in frustration without divine help.

When we open ourselves to the guidance of the Holy Spirit, God uses us as His instruments to help others.

And as God's peace flows through us to others, we also are filled with greater peace.

◄ ►

The Lord is in His holy temple;
let all the earth
keep silence before Him.
— Habakkuk 2:20

Touching God isn't a matter of exploration in the vast world beyond. It's more a return to the self, the deepest self.

There's no need to fuss about reaching out to Divine Life as though God were infinitely distant.

We are always in God's Presence.

The instant we reflect on His abiding Presence in us, we become conscious of our union with Him, and that is the beginning of prayer.

Once you understand this, you have only to consider who it is that abides in you and with you.

The Gospels tell us that God is always faithful and that God is always present to us as a lover who seeks to support and sustain us.

As Lent begins, allow the Lord to guide and direct you in becoming a more loving person.

◀ ▶

March 2

In the world you have tribulation;
but be of good cheer,
I have overcome the world.
— John 16:33

I'd like to take a little poll. It will be a private poll between you and me. How would you answer these questions:

Do you believe in God?

Is He a distant God or do you feel that He's close to you?

Do you believe that God is Love and that God desires to be close to you?

I hope so because it's all true.

God is a loving Father and there's no need to strain to reach Him. He longs to be united with you, just as Jesus longed to reach out to those in need, to the poor, and the sick. His compassion toward the ordinary people of His day is a reflection of His Father's unchanging love for all of us.

> *Know the love of Christ*
> *that surpasses all knowledge.*
> — *Ephesians 3:19*

"As I grow older, my need for Jesus grows stronger. I have become more independent within myself, but more dependent on Jesus. It is He who molds me and makes me who I am.

"Jesus is constantly on my mind. Perhaps He is not always at the forefront of my thoughts, but He is there, waiting in the shadows for me to acknowledge Him.

"Sometimes if I act too recklessly, or speak too sharply, it is then that Jesus reminds me that the gesture I made or the words I have spoken are not in keeping with the teachings of the One whom I have promised to love above all else.

"So now, before I make a move I ask myself, 'Would you do this or say that if Jesus were standing before you in the flesh?'

"Yet Jesus does know what I do. He is closer than my own flesh. He is Spirit dwelling within me. He forgives me. And always, He loves me."
— R.K., Horse Shoe, NC

◄ ►

*Why are you cast down, O my soul,
and why are you disquieted within me?
Hope in God.*
— *Psalm 42:5*

There is a story about the devil displaying the various tools his followers should use to mislead humans. The impressive array included Pride, Hatred, Jealousy, Dishonesty, Impurity.

Beside these large tools a small, less noticeable one was displayed.

"What's the name of this one," a devil asked, "and of what use can it be?"

"Oh," replied Satan, "a most valuable instrument, I assure you. It always works when the others fail. I call it Discouragement."

One of the devil's cleverest tricks is to dishearten people to such an extent that they take the attitude: "Why should I knock myself out when nobody else cares?"

Anyone who would be a Christ-bearer must expect to be tempted by discouragement. St. Francis de Sales once said, "Don't be discouraged if you're discouraged." In other words, laugh at yourself and keep on going.

◀ ▶

(Daniel) got down upon his knees
three times a day and prayed and
gave thanks before God.
— Daniel 6:10

Prayer is basically giving yourself to God. The only way to pray well is to give yourself to God often — sometimes while you're on the run, and at other times when you settle down to really communicate with the Lord.

In learning how to pray, try to remember two things. First, prayer is not so much what you do, as what you stop doing. You have to stop running around in order to open yourself to God's loving Presence.

At prayer time try to relax your mind and body. Sit still. Control your body as your way of giving yourself to God.

Second, you shouldn't imagine that good prayer always results in good feelings. God does not grade you according to your emotional feelings of solace and comfort. He simply wants the opportunity to offer Himself to you as you quietly try to offer yourself to Him.

If you make a reasonable offer to trust your entire life to God's gentle care, all will be well.

◀ ▶

*I waited patiently for the Lord, He inclined to
me and heard my cry ... He set my feet
upon a rock, making my steps secure.
He put a new song in my mouth,
a song of praise to our God.*
— *Psalm 40:1-3*

We all need more faith, courage, and enthusiasm. A hopeful attitude can be a great blessing
in times of trouble.

On the contrary, a despairing or apathetic attitude deprives you of joy and at the same time
discourages everyone around you.

Hope is rooted in the knowledge of God's love
which Jesus revealed so emphatically. When you're
sustained by hope, you draw power and determination from your unseen Lover, and He gives
you a new song to sing.

Whenever you try to bring your light into the
darkness, you help make this a better world.

◀ ▶

*We have peace with God through our
Lord Jesus Christ. Through Him we
have obtained access to this grace
in which we stand.*
— *Romans 5:1-2*

"By Grace I have come to experience with profound consolation the true knowledge and assurance that God and His plan of salvation and all of His awesome attributes are the same as they were before the beginning, are now and will be forever and ever.

"My situations, mistakes, circumstances, weaknesses, attitudes and sins can all be used for His glory as long as I am faithful in trusting Him with sincerity and good will.

"Throughout my life the religion of the commandments was my banner — I couldn't quite get a handle on the Beatitudes so I lived a life of quiet desperation, hidden frustration, and a not-so-hidden harshness of attitudes.

"After years of reading books on self-improvement and psychology, God opened a Way so I could hear His Truth. He simply poured His Love into my heart during prayer when I sincerely promised to be available for His purposes all the days of my life. That was 16 years ago. He still keeps me in His Grace."

— A.S., River Edge, NJ

◀ ▶

*All the ends of the earth shall remember
and turn to the Lord.*
— *Psalm 22:27*

Isaac Bashevis Singer, whose stories have charmed readers for three generations, once explained his views on prayer:

"Whenever I'm in trouble, I pray. And since I'm always in trouble, there is not a day when I don't pray. The belief that we can do what we want, without God, is as far from me as the North Pole."

Pollution, war, racial and political conflict — these and other pressing issues have placed our entire planet in jeopardy. Solutions must be sought, in our relationships with others and with the loving Creator who sustains us in being.

By taking three minutes a day for prayerful reflection, more if you can, can bring more energy and insight to the job that only you can do today.

◀ ▶

> *Listen to me in silence, O coastlands.*
> — *Isaiah 41:1*

Contemplation is simply gazing upon the Lord, while absorbing His love.

Without words, or thoughts or symbols, gazing upon the Lord brings great peace.

Contemplation is essentially the spiritual enjoyment of God. It is called the Prayer of Silence.

It is a beautiful prayer in which you do nothing, think nothing, say nothing.

You do not always have to engage God directly or consciously with words or thoughts. You can from time to time just absorb the sights and sounds and smells around you. God is in all of these things.

Silence is God's natural dwelling place.

Silence is God's language.

> *Owe no one anything,*
> *except to love one another;*
> *for the one who loves another*
> *has fulfilled the law.*
> — *Romans 13:8*

Lives change when people care.

We all need to be loved, to be valued, to be told that we're worthwhile.

Would you try something today? Tell someone in your life — a child or an adult, a family member or a friend — that they're really special to you. Tell them you feel lucky to know them, that you love them just the way they are.

God loves each of us — just the way we are.

Maybe we can do a little more to show that love to others every day.

◀ ▶

> *(Jesus) said to him, "Follow Me."*
> *And (Matthew) got up, left everything,*
> *and followed Him.*
> — *Luke 5:27*

"Growing up in the 1950's attending Catholic school, I saw Jesus as a tragic, pain-filled figure on a cross whom I had caused enormous suffering. I felt I was a terrible person.

"As I reached young adulthood, for a time I pushed Him out of my life. Why did I want to think of so much suffering? Life was terribly hard with my parents both ill, a child to rear. Money was short. I prayed sporadically, but I pushed it all away. Why add pain to pain?

"In 1978, through my sister's guidance and Divine Intervention, I discovered the charismatic movement. I approached it gingerly and curiously. For the first time Christ was love, joy, happiness and yes, pain, too. But this pain was tolerable and even embraceable!

"A year later, I underwent a mastectomy and my life turned around. I was hooked on Jesus' mercy, loving protection and Master Plan.

"Today I am well. I praise Him daily and pray to learn to love Him more. There is a serenity in my life. He doesn't frighten me any longer."

— B.K., Tampa, FL

◀ ▶

The meditation of my heart
shall be understanding.
— Psalm 49:3

Erich Fromm, the psychoanalyst, was once asked for a practical solution to the problems of living.

"Quietness," he answered. "The experience of stillness. You have to stop in order to change direction." This of course is true if you ever want to pray.

Meditation, the kind of reflection we do when we're alone, creates a "quiet place" in our lives. It removes us from everyday "busyness" so that we can concentrate on what is going on inside. It removes us from competing claims for our attention, so that we can get more in touch with what we feel, think, and believe.

Meditation sometimes is a kind of daydreaming in the Lord. It can help us see God's will as it is revealed to us in the events of everyday life. And it can bring us increased strength, serenity and understanding.

◄ ►

> *When you pray, go into your room*
> *and shut the door and pray*
> *to your Father . . . and your Father*
> *who sees in secret will reward you.*
> *— Matthew 6:6*

Develop a taste for relaxed, open and honest communication.

You need to accept yourself and at the same time believe that God accepts you.

Then you can gently ask for the grace of holiness, the grace of transformation in Christ Jesus.

Christ said ask and you will receive. Why not take Him at His word?

Ask for the gift of relaxed, open and honest communication. Don't stop there. Ask also for self-acceptance, holiness, and finally for the gift of transformation in Christ.

◄ ►

*I am the Lord . . . I have taken you by the hand
and kept you. I have given you as a covenant
to the people, a light to the nations,
to open the eyes that are blind, to bring out
the prisoners from the dungeon, from the
prison those who sit in darkness.*
— *Isaiah 42:6-7*

Jesus referred to this text as a prophecy of His ministry.

What does the word vocation mean to you? Literally, it comes from the Latin word vocare, to call. A vocation is a calling from God. Jesus was called by God and so are you.

It would be wrong to imagine that only priests or those in religious life have a calling from God. Each and every one of us is called by God to use our gifts and our talents for the good of others.

In choosing a profession, in committing to marriage, in striving to be a good parent, and countless other ways we have an opportunity to respond to God's call: To live our lives as an instrument of His love.

God invites each of us to serve Him by serving our neighbor.

◀ ▶

As a mother comforts her child,
so I will comfort you.
— Isaiah 66:13

"One afternoon, in church, Jesus revealed Himself in an unseen yet intimate way. Jesus promised He would always love me. At that moment, He became my life-long best friend. It was not unusual, then, to spend some of my lunch time chatting with Him heart-to-heart even as I munched on a candy bar.

"As I grow older and become more aware of my limitations, I also seem to become more aware of His strength which upholds me, His companionship in my widowhood and His ever-present love revealed through supportive family and wonderful friends. I know He will be there for me at the moment of death and I so look forward to seeing Him face to face.

"I wish everyone could grasp how much they are loved by so gentle a God. His love is everywhere: in the warm hot chocolate on a cold day, in the hug of a friend, in the compliment of husband or wife, even in those difficult moments that remind us of our need for Him. Ultimately Jesus is for me the Person I can help and the One who helps me."

— C.K., Orlando, FL

◄ ►

(The Lord) gave skill to human beings
that He might be glorified
in His marvelous works.
— Sirach 38:6

Professor Abraham Maslow used to challenge students with questions like: "Which of you is going to write the next novel?" "Who is going to be a saint like Schweitzer?"

Confronted with such big ideas, the students would only blush, squirm and giggle. Then the famed psychologist would assure them that he meant what he said.

"If not you, who will?" he demanded. We could each ask that question of ourselves. Blind chance didn't put us here. A loving God did, as part of His plan for creation. We are not given to know the total design of God's master plan.

But each day that dawns reveals a portion of that plan. At each moment, God holds out a chance for us to be more, to achieve more. Each moment He gives us what we need to respond to His loving invitation.

We have what it takes. Will we use it? If not us, then who?

◀ ▶

> *Blessed be the Lord*
> *who has given rest to His people.*
> — *Kings 8:56*

There can be no enjoyment of the Lord without a spirit at rest.

Relax. Try to become comfortable. Let yourself go.

God is always present to you. His Presence means infinite, unchanging love. Trust Him. Be with Him. Receive from Him. Imagine Him caring for you. Do not measure your success or failure. Just go to Him.

Can such a labor, day after day, be pleasing to God? Yes. Even if the whole time is filled with inner noise and distraction one can have the joy of consciously offering one's self to God.

God does not grade your prayer, giving you an "A" when you feel cozy about it. Avoid all such delusions and just learn to relax. Use your mood swings as prayer, even if they are uncomfortable. Sooner or later you will understand that your daily prayer is you, giving yourself to God. The experience of quiet joy might follow but don't bank on it. Just give your daily experiences.

Lift them up to your Lord and all will be well.

◀ ▶

> *A faithful friend is a sturdy shelter:*
> *whoever has found one*
> *has found a treasure.*
> — *Sirach 6:14*

Friendship is the comfort of feeling safe in the company of another person.

Friendship is talking, laughing, crying and playing together — the sharing of ideas and experiences.

However you define friendship, its essence is daring to love and to be loved.

In loving each other, we reflect the source of all love.

Thank God for the gift of friendship.

◄ ►

"Why were you searching for Me?
Did you not know that I must be
in My Father's house?"
— Luke 2:49

"I am 47 years old. My son, an only child, is twenty and going to college. I was born in the Philippines and came to this country 21 years ago. Before my wife got seriously ill and passed away I considered myself a 'Sunday Catholic.' I was bored, but 'they' were religious fanatics and I wasn't.

"For the first time in my life I started to search for Jesus Christ. I longed for His presence. I asked people about Him. I read books and magazines about Him. I listened to music. I joined our choir. I read the Bible. I learned to say the rosary. I simply thirst for the Living Water. He is there within my heart. He was there all the time waiting for me to sense His presence and come into His fold.

"He gave me peace of mind. I asked forgiveness from friends and relatives. My son and I are beginning to analyze what causes our relationship to sour sometimes.

"Each new day seems always to be brighter."
— J.P., Channelview, TX

◄ ►

Love never ends.
— *1 Corinthians 13:8*

Mark Twain, in a whimsical mood, once said: "Let us endeavor so to live that when we come to die, even the undertaker will be sorry."

People who are most lovable in this life and most sorely missed after they die are those who have sincerely tried to make the world better for their being in it. In a way they start their heaven on earth.

Cram your life with acts of love for God and your fellow human beings. Remember that our mission in life is a happy journey back to a loving Father, even though it means hard work.

Keep trying to perfect your love for your Maker and all humankind and you will develop a heavenly quality that endures through death and into eternity.

◄ ►

*This is love, not that we loved God
but that He loved us and sent His Son
to be the expiation for our sins.*
— 1 John 4:10

All prayer is vain if it does not help you to love.
To love, you must accept yourself.

And to accept yourself, you must understand
that you are an ordinary human being.

Even though you may fall from time to time
you know that God loves you. He needs your
hands, your voice and your heart to minister His
saving love to others.

Self-acceptance is the first sign of healthy and
proper self-love. From this starting point it becomes reasonable to accept and eventually love
your neighbor. You cannot deal charitably with
the faults of someone else if you cannot accept
your own faults. Conversely, you can better accept others with all their failings once you have
come to terms with your own.

Until you accept yourself, nothing grows.

God never changes in His love for you, but
unless you realize that, your prayer will be full of
frustration.

◄ ►

Before Jesus said to the paralytic, *Take up your bed and walk,* He said, *Take heart, Friend, your sins are forgiven.* (Luke 5:24, 20)

Healing and forgiveness are continually combined in the Gospels.

Each one of us is paralyzed until we accept — really accept — the fact that God forgives us.

Once we do, we are not only freed from guilt, we are freed to love, to believe in ourselves and to forgive those who injure us.

Healing and forgiveness are the constant message of Jesus.

And healing and forgiveness is a way of life.

◄ ►

March 23

From the rising of the sun
to its setting
the name of the Lord
is to be praised.
— Psalm 113:3

"Jesus Christ is my daily life. Yet while under covers or before covering for sleep, my first and last words are for my Lord.

"I am the most imperfect of His saints, yet He chose me for His work of showing everyone that I love Him, believe in Him and trust Him. Every minute I depend on Jesus Christ.

"After five strokes my writing cannot catch up with my thoughts. Please forgive me, but I know that my Lord and my God will help you understand what I am trying to convey to you — the deep love I have for Him.

"Every time I say, 'My Lord and my God, help me,' He truly does."

— P.C., Redding, CA

◄ ►

> *Let us run with perseverance*
> *the race set before us.*
> *— Hebrews 12:1*

Have you ever wondered why seasoned anglers never give up?

Of all explanations, this seems best:

"There are two reasons for the proverbial persistence of anglers. The first is that the fish are biting; the second is that they are not. Either is sufficient justification for fishing a little longer."

Anyone who tries to be of a genuine service to others — in the home, the neighborhood, or in public life — eventually gets discouraged, feeling, "What's the use?"

The Lord who sustains you when "the fish are biting" blesses you even more when you don't get so much as a nibble.

◀ ▶

*The angel said to her, "Do not be afraid,
Mary, for you have found favor with God.
And now, you will conceive in your
womb and bear a son, and you will name
Him Jesus. He will be great, and will be
called the Son of the Most High."*
— Luke 1:30-32

When the Holy Spirit came to Mary she was
not asked to renounce anything, or to travel far
away on a great mission, or to enter a monastery.

Mary was asked to carry Christ.

That's just what God asks of each one of us
— to be a Christopher — to carry Christ into the
world.

For a rich, fulfilled life, there are three things
you have to do: one, cling to God. Clinging to
God is the essence of prayer.

Two, think of others — that's charity. Thinking of others will save you a lot of self-centered
anxiety.

Three, don't put yourself down. Try to be your
own best friend. Life will be a lot more joyful.

◄ ►

If you love to listen
you will gain knowledge,
and if you incline your ear
you will become wise.
— *Sirach 6:33*

We listen — that we might hear. We listen — that we might better understand.

There are many barriers to communication besides physical ones. A lack of time, a lack of sensitivity or a lack of interest.

Still, each event in our lives, every person we meet, gives us an opportunity to communicate warmth, concern and, yes, even love.

God created us out of His love. He put us into this world to share it with us.

Through love, we become connected with others — and with Him — sometimes without speaking a word.

◀ ▶

> *We suffer with Him so that*
> *we may also be glorified with Him.*
> — *Romans 8:17*

"I was sitting in church anxiously seeking Him. I wanted to lay my tremendous burden at his feet. I had schizophrenic sons I didn't know how to cope with. Silent tears rolled down my face. I wiped them away. They reappeared. I quickly looked around to see if anyone noticed. They didn't, and the tears kept flowing. I felt at peace and cleansed. Then, suddenly, an electric field surrounded me. The touch of Jesus! I knew this at a deep level. He left as swiftly as He came leaving me forever changed.

"Ever since, I have thought of Jesus as my connection between this world and the next. My sons have improved and found a place for themselves although they are not cured. I can bear this burden because I know that Jesus knows and cares. It strengthened me through yet another trial to come when I found out my daughter was an alcoholic. I prayed my heart out and He answered. She is recovering and now helps others.

"I'm happy in the midst of suffering I share with Jesus because He surrounds me with His love."

— M.C., Micanopy, FL

◀ ▶

> *The Lord said to Abram,*
> *"Go from your country and*
> *your kindred and your father's house*
> *to the land that I will show you."*
> — *Genesis 12:1*

I seem to be always at some kind of crossroads, Lord.

I start down one road. And it forks. Or I find out I took a wrong turn and have to go back and start again.

Why so many decisions, Lord? Why so few maps or signposts?

I know. My life is unique, uncharted. It's a path no one has ever taken, so there's no travel guide.

A long time ago, You told Abram: to go to *the land that I will show you.*

You tell every child born into this world the same thing. You show us the way in the people, circumstances and events of everyday life. And every decision we make is a step on that journey of faith — faith in You and faith in ourselves because You have made us.

Guide our feet in the right paths, Lord.

Amen.

◄ ►

> *Has the Lord as great delight*
> *in burnt offerings and sacrifices,*
> *as in obeying the voice of the Lord?*
> *Behold, to obey is better than sacrifice.*
> — *1 Samuel 15:22*

Before getting down on yourself for not realizing your dream of perfection, find out if your dream is from God.

Don't waste energy praying for something extraordinary that God doesn't want for you. He loves ordinary people. People who bite their nails, people who exaggerate, people who are overweight, people who smoke too much, people who have erotic thoughts, even people who steal and murder.

God never despises the sinner. Learn to see yourself as the Lord sees you — through the eyes of love.

It is the work of the devil to fill you with the thought that you are worthless, rejected, despised. Don't believe it. Don't be anxious about your faults and failings or about God's love for you. God loves you just as you are. He knows how to make you His instrument. He knows how to bring you to His own radiant glory.

◄ ►

Depart from evil, and do good;
so shall you abide for ever.
— *Psalm 37:27*

How can we make this world a better place?
Well, by being an instrument of God's peace and
love.

God has endowed each one of us with a spark
of greatness, which is given to us for the enrich-
ment of others. To allow that spark of greatness to burn brightly within you, you must first
learn how to accept and develop those God-given
gifts which are uniquely yours.

A lovely singing voice, for instance, certainly
can enhance the world, but we can't all be world
class singers. The nice thing is that we don't have
to be world class anything. We just have to be
ourselves, and to make good use of the gifts that
we've been given.

Perhaps you are good with children, or an excellent writer, or a great problem-solver, or a wonderful cook. The Scriptures tell us that the most important gift of all is charity, which includes kindness, reliability, patience, cheerfulness, and perseverance.

The gifts you share with others can make the
world around you a much happier place. So never
doubt your power to overcome evil with good.

◀ ▶

*Those who plan good
find loyalty and faithfulness.*
— Proverbs 14:22

"Who is Jesus Christ in my life? He is my way
of life. My thinking, working, playing all are gifts
from Him. Each day I try to resemble Him in little
acts of kindness. Nothing great comes my way to
offer. However, as I grow He reveals to me that
loving is in the giving. The size of the gift we offer
is enlarged in proportion to the love we offer in
His name, not by the size of the deed.

"The Holy Eucharist is His gift to us and the
closest contact I can have with my God. To place
Himself in our hands speaks of His extravagant
love for His human family. Here in the sanctuary
of our hearts He whispers, 'Love Me. Be My
Hands, Feet, Eyes. Reach out to others and then
you will resemble Me.'

"I delight in the knowledge that when I say I'll
try harder tomorrow He smiles on me. Sleep
comes peacefully because He is my best friend
who loves me in spite of failures. Perhaps tomorrow I'll resemble my Father more."

— M.D., Manchester, NH

◀ ▶

April 1

They shall obtain joy and gladness;
sorrow and sighing shall flee away.
— *Isaiah 35:10*

Generally speaking, people who are able to sense God's love in their lives are happy people. Being happy and having a sense of humor are traits that can help lighten some of life's burdens.

Remember how good it felt the last time you enjoyed a hearty laugh? Happiness is what God wants for each one of us. We were created for an eternity of happiness.

In the words of Blessed Julian of Norwich, "The greatest honor you can give almighty God is to live gladly because of the knowledge of His love."

◀ ▶

*The eyes of the Lord are upon those
who love Him, a mighty protection and
strong support, a shelter from the hot wind
and a shade from the noonday sun,
a guard against stumbling and
a defense against falling.
He . . . gives light to the eyes;
He grants healing, life and blessing.*
— *Sirach 34:16-17*

God is Love. It is His joy to be with you. Begin to know the personal joy of being with Him.

Find the time to be alone with God to enjoy His Presence. Your praise and thanksgiving can be a warm and happy expression of joy.

Silence is also a beautiful expression of joy.

You need to speak to God, but you also need to listen to God. You need to receive more and more of His power and tenderness by forgetting yourself and listening to Him. God may not talk to you in a human voice, but you will hear Him and know of His eternal love.

Prayer is the act of adverting to the reality of His love. It is enjoying all that God wishes to give on a particular. Prayer is food for the spirit. Prayer is receiving something essential to life, namely spiritual joy.

◄ ►

April 3

In the morning, while it was still very dark,
(Jesus) got up and went out to a deserted place,
and there He prayed.
— Mark 1:35

Sometimes the hardest thing about prayer is stopping everything else. This is where the will comes in. Don't wait until you have some pressing need, or until you're in the proper frame of mind. If you do that, you may go days without praying. When the time you've chosen for prayer comes, stop whatever you're doing and give yourself to God in your own way.

For those who like to begin their day with prayer, here is the morning prayer of Mother Teresa and her co-workers:

"I have come to Thee to take Thy touch before I begin my day.

"Let Your eyes rest upon my eyes for a while.

"Let me take to my work the assurance of Your friendship.

"Fill my mind so it will last through the desert of noise.

"Let Your blessed sunshine fill the peaks of my thoughts. And give me strength for those who need me.

"Amen."

◄ ►

The Lord is my strength and my song,
and He has become my salvation.
— *Exodus 15:2*

"I married a man at 19, raised six children. He was abusive, physically, mentally, and spiritually. He told me to get out after 33 years of marriage because I had changed! My marriage was annulled. He wanted to be my god.

"Who rescued me? Guess? Our Lord Jesus Christ. He is my Peace and consolation and Joy.

"Everything I have is from Him. The good that I do is because of Him. I love Him, but He loves me even more.

"I know that He is always with me. I ask Him to bless my children and His children and He does. He fills me with His grace and Holy Spirit and He enlightens me."

— M.N., Milford, MA

◄ ►

April 5

> *Brothers and sisters,*
> *do not be weary*
> *in doing what is right.*
> — *2 Thessalonians 3:13*

One person can make a difference.

Individuals have the capacity not only to change lives but to affect the flow of history. Too often people underestimate their own power to do some far-reaching good.

Sacred Scripture calls us to be a light in this world of darkness.

Remember, a journey of a thousand miles begins with the first step.

You can begin to be a light, a carrier of divine love and divine truth right where you are, right now, right in your own home.

◀ ▶

*Let my prayer be counted as incense
before You, and the lifting up of my hands
as an evening sacrifice.*
— *Psalm 141:2*

Teach yourself to have a good attitude about
your own body, however imperfect it may be.
Those who hate their body attack themselves un-
fairly. Every human body is an amazing creation
of God's genius.

It is not enough for you to know that there is
nothing dirty or evil about the human body. You
must appreciate that it is good, beautifully designed, integrated in its operations, useful, well-
conformed. It is to your body that resurrection
has been promised.

It is not enough to say that you love your own
body. You must also realize that you love it.

Offer to God the homage of your being just
as you are. Please Him by not complaining about
the gifts He has given you.

Love your own body even if you are sickly for
your body has enabled you to live a human life.
In all circumstances be grateful to God.

◀ ▶

> *Jesus . . . said to him,*
> *"Follow Me."*
> — *Matthew 9:9*

Jesus attracted many followers. They didn't all understand why they followed Him. Most of them did not want to be disturbed in their day-to-day routine. They were not always comfortable with His words. And yet, because of Him, they experienced a change within themselves. They began to think about their destiny in a new way.

Follow Me, He said. And they followed. They were fearful, hesitant and, by the world's standards, unsuitable for the challenge put before them.

We are like them. It's hard for us to be optimistic about changing a world so filled with evil influences. But the Lord convinced His followers that with the help of God they could move mountains. And gradually they did. By letting the Spirit fill them they became a mighty force. Gradually they overcame the hostile power of the Roman Empire.

We, too, have a destiny to be victorious over evil. As bearers of divine love and wisdom, together we can change the world.

◀ ▶

> *I will see you again*
> *and your hearts will rejoice,*
> *and no one*
> *will take your joy from you.*
> *— John 16:22*

The word "joy" is mentioned in the Bible more than 130 times. God wants us to lead lives that are truly joyous. As Dom Marmion said, "Joy is the echo of God's life within us."

But the Lord's concept of joy is quite different from what the world calls pleasure.

Joy is of the heart, the mind, and the soul. It has a deep and lasting quality that can carry a person through hardship and suffering.

Pleasure, on the other hand, is usually connected with physical delight. It can be fleeting and even joyless when pursued for its own sake.

Seek the true joy that comes from the Lord, and you will never be separated from His love.

◀ ▶

God the Lord is my strength;
He makes my feet like the feet of a deer,
and makes me tread upon the heights.
— Habakkuk 3:19

Have you ever wanted to give up? Or gotten so tired that you didn't want to try anymore, and you felt like you couldn't find the strength to go on?

At times like these you realize that you need something more. That your own limited strength just isn't enough.

When that moment comes, don't despair. There is always grace and light and strength from above, and it's yours for the asking.

Jesus walked the path of pain and darkness. He knows your pain. Invite Him into your life and accept His comforting love.

◄ ►

*The Father is in Me
and I am in the Father.*
— John 10:38

For Jesus, the Father was everything. His whole purpose, motivation and activity was directed to Him. Jesus had come to do His Father's will. Jesus was a man for others but only in the sense that the Father had sent Him to save humankind. He was more a man for the Father.

Knowing this, we try to imitate Jesus by our devotion to the Father's will. Jesus told us to keep it simple.

Be as trusting as a child. At the same time be careful that you don't fool yourself, deciding what you want and then convincing yourself it's what God wants. Be open to the Spirit.

Learn to imitate Jesus' abandonment to the Father's loving care. Trust the past to His mercy and the future to His Divine Providence.

◄ ►

> *Peace I leave with you;*
> *My peace I give to you.*
> *— John 14:27*

In giving us His peace, Jesus assures us that peace is possible — even in the midst of turmoil and suffering.

How are we to attain this peace which is beyond all understanding? By bringing peace to others — by becoming instruments of Christ's peace.

Kent Evans did not know Dawn, a woman attempting to cope with the death of her loving husband. Nevertheless, he wrote to console her when he learned of her grief. "Let Ralph live on in your heart," he said. "Everyone who knew him will know his presence in you."

Kent Evans was writing from a prison in Richmond, Virginia, where he was serving a life sentence.

Whoever, wherever you are, you, too, are meant to be an instrument of God's peace.

◄ ►

April 12

Do not weep for Me,
but weep for yourselves
and for your children.
— Luke 23:28

"What a wonderful gift we have been given, all of us in tune, loving and being loved by the greatest lover of all, Christ.

"You have but to review His passion and death, His dignity when facing Pilate. His humility when accepting the cross. His bravery when falling and rising to go on.

"His awful love when meeting His mother. The anguish of Our Lady when Christ at last dies. His work is done.

"This is Jesus in my life, and at Mass when I receive Him I know that He will always be my friend, my love, my redeemer."

— E.H., Delray, FL

◀ ▶

*We boast in our sufferings
knowing that suffering produces endurance,
and endurance produces character,
and character produces hope,
and hope does not disappoint us
because God's love has been
poured into our hearts.*
— *Romans 5: 3-5*

Suffering is an unavoidable part of life. Sometimes we have no real choice about it.

But we do have a choice about the way we face suffering.

We can endure unavoidable suffering grudgingly and resentfully, or we can accept the inevitable and try to live our lives around it, finding happiness where we can. This is called cheerful acquiescence.

None of us are really alone in our troubles. God's strength works in and through us. In our weakness we have to learn to rely on the power of Almighty God.

So lift up your heart and have a new confidence. Let today be a day of gratitude and cheer. With God's help all things are possible.

◀ ▶

For a brief moment I forsook you,
but with great compassion I will gather you.
In overflowing wrath for a moment
I hid My face from you, but with
everlasting love I will have compassion
on you, says the Lord, your Redeemer.
— Isaiah 54:7-8

The Resurrection of Jesus was preceded by pain. As terrible as that pain was, it was a saving pain. Suffering is the coin that purchased our redemption.

God *does* draw good from evil. He *does* write straight with crooked lines. He is bringing us to glory and happiness.

The dominant theme of life is hopeful, full of promise, and for this we are grateful.

Can we trust the Crucified Savior? Can we believe that His death will bring about our eternal bliss? We can, with all the power and strength of our being.

But faith requires more than mere intellectual assent. It calls for the decision to accept Jesus, the Christ, as our personal Redeemer and it requires our loving gratitude.

◄ ►

*Even though I walk through
the valley of the shadow of death,
I fear no evil;
for You are with me.*
— *Psalm 23:4*

This prayer of St. Augustine will help prepare your heart for Easter.

"God of life,
"there are days when the burdens we carry chafe our shoulders and wear us down,

"when the road seems dreary and endless, the skies grey and threatening;

"when our lives have no music in them, our hearts are lonely, and our souls have lost their courage.

"Flood the path with light, we beseech Thee Lord, turn our eyes to where the heavens are full of promise."

◀ ▶

We have our hope set on the living God,
who is the Savior of all people.
— 1 Timothy 4:10

Here are the opening words of an Easter sermon preached by St. John Chrysostom, patriarch of Constantinople in the fourth century.

"Let us celebrate this greatest and most shining feast, in which the Lord has risen from the dead.

"Let us celebrate it with joy, and in equal measure with devotion.

"For the Lord has risen, and together with Him He has raised the whole world. He has risen, because He has broken the bonds of death."

This great Doctor of the Church concludes with a promise of eternal happiness for those who serve God.

"May it be granted to each one of us to reach (eternal) happiness, through the grace and mercy of Our Lord Jesus Christ, to Whom, with the Father and the Holy Ghost, be (all) glory and adoration, world without end. Amen."

◀ ▶

I rise before dawn and cry for help . . .
my eyes are awake before each watch
of the night, that I may
meditate on Your promise.
— Psalm 119:147,148

A construction worker describes the beginning of each day:

"I rise at 5:45 a.m. I make the Sign of the Cross, thank and praise the Lord for a new day and then bless my wife and each child, starting with the eldest, a fifteen-year-old, down to the youngest, a two-year-old. We have been blessed with nine beautiful children, and they aren't accidents. My wife and I love each one dearly. I am most grateful to God for all His blessings.

"I spend a half hour reading the Bible. I think about God's words.

"I then go off to Mass.

"Following Communion, and after a few moments of thanksgiving I go off to work thinking about the Lord's presence within me."

This man indeed rises *before dawn and . . . meditate(s) on Your promise.* Something for the rest of us to ponder.

◄ ►

Jesus told them a parable
about their need to pray always . . .
There was a judge who neither feared God
nor had respect for people . . .
a widow kept coming to him and saying:
"Grant me justice against my opponent."
For a while he refused; but later he said . . .
"Though I have no fear of God and no respect
for anyone, yet because this widow
keeps bothering me, I will grant her justice,
so that she may not wear me out" . . .
will not God grant justice to His chosen ones
who cry to Him day and night? . . . I tell you,
He will quickly grant justice to them.
— Luke 18:1,2,3-5,7,8

Here we see Jesus encouraging us to be persistent in prayer and to have faith that God is listening.

There are many who have never thought of themselves as being very prayerful but for years they have repeated short prayers to suit their needs.

They have developed a simple, direct line to God. They live constantly in God's presence.

They may not feel very spiritual, but they are.

What is important is that they have learned to pray with persistence.

◀ ▶

*Go therefore and make disciples
of all nations ... teaching them to obey
everything that I have commanded you.
— Matthew 28:19,20*

A believer and a skeptic went for a walk.

The skeptic said, "Look at the trouble and misery in the world after thousands of years of religion. What good is religion?"

His companion noticed a child, filthy with grime, playing in the gutter. He said, "We've had soap for generation after generation yet look how dirty that child is. Of what value is soap?"

The skeptic protested, "But soap can't do any good unless it is used!"

"Exactly," replied the believer.

Let your faith shine out for all to see. Don't bury it because you live in a pluralistic society. Be who you are. Let your faith be a light for those around you, skeptics and all.

◀ ▶

*Lead me to the rock that is higher than I,
for You are my refuge.*
— *Psalm 61:2-3*

"Jesus Christ is a guiding light, the son of God, and my best friend.

"He entered my life when I was a child. Then He was a gentleman that kept scary things away when I called His name, He gave me courage to lift my head from beneath the blankets to face the darkness. He covered me in warmth and gentleness when the world about me was cruel and harsh.

"He gifted me with the talent and patience to be a good listener and advisor. He gifted me with the ability to help other children through their difficulties. Through these experiences I found my calling in life.

"I help and guide others with Jesus at my side. As He leads, I shall follow for He's seen me through very tough times, and I know He'll be there in my tomorrow."

— T.Z., Joliet, IL

◄ ►

April 21

May all who seek You rejoice
and be glad in You;
may those who love Your salvation
say continually, "Great is the Lord!"
— Psalm 40:16

The Christophers' material is read all across the United States and in dozens of countries around the world. This means that there are probably Catholics, Protestants, Jews, Muslims, Buddhists, Hindus and people of other religions who will read this book.

The fact is, we are all very different from one another yet we believe in exactly the same God, since there is only one God. We may travel different paths to reach Him, but there is only one destination.

The sacred books of every religion teach their followers to love and respect others. We are all children of the same loving Father.

Let us love one another.

◀ ▶

> *Stand every morning,*
> *thanking and praising the Lord,*
> *and likewise at evening.*
> — *1 Chronicles 23:30*

We are not always attracted to prayer. There are times when we know only numbness and inertia, but these are moments when we meet God in desolation. Don't be discouraged with your lack of consistency. St. Therese of Lisieux said, "When I am in such a state . . . I say very slowly the 'Our Father' or the 'Hail Mary.'"

Prayer is enjoying life, enjoying music, enjoying work; it is giving and receiving love.

Yet, while this is true, it is important to develop some pattern of prayer. This is a good way to insure that you will gather yourself together on a fairly regular basis before your Lord, whether you are in peace or in turmoil.

Faithfulness does not mean that you will always feel the same about your prayer.

Accept that. Accept your humanness. Especially at prayer.

Faithfulness means you give yourself to God both on good days and bad.

◄ ►

Beloved, let us love one another,
because love is from God; everyone who
loves . . . knows God.
— 1 John 4:7

O God, unite our hearts in the never-ending bond of pure love.

May our children bring You happiness and may Your generous love for them be returned to You many times over.

May the peace of Christ live always in our heart and in our home.

May we have true friends who stand by us in joy and in sorrow.

May we be ready to help and comfort all who come to us in need, and may the blessings promised to the compassionate someday be ours.

May we find happiness and satisfaction in our occupations.

May daily problems never cause us undue anxiety, nor the desire for earthly comforts dominate our lives.

May our hearts' first desire always be the hundredfold promised to Your faithful people.

And may You one day welcome us together into Your eternal kingdom.

Amen

◀ ▶

> *He is before all things,*
> *and in Him all things hold together.*
> — *Colossians 1:17*

"One day I was standing at a bus stop. A promoter of the Gospel came toward me and asked, 'Have you seen Jesus?' I was able to reply, 'Yes, I have.' This is my story.

"I saw the Risen Christ Jesus. He walked with me — not beside me, but in me. At that quiet time I experienced the integration of Jesus and little me. We were one. I tested this revelation, not sure it was real. Was I imagining this?

"In time I saw it was a special grace that would affect the rest of my life. The Risen Christ Jesus whom we receive in the Eucharist is He who conquers death, despair, destruction.

"Each time I sense failure or feel overwhelmed, I remember the lesson Jesus taught me. I rise again with new strength and stand taller with the knowledge that faith cuts through lethargy, that hope banishes fear of the future and that Love Himself is always there, as close as my heartbeat.

"With Him I can reach out to others with sensitivity and compassion, for together, as we return to the Father, we are made whole."

— L.D., Cambridge, MA

◄ ►

April 25

The Lord has heard
the sound of my weeping.
The Lord has heard my supplication;
the Lord accepts my prayer.
— *Psalm 6:8-9*

The Lord is our friend. And a friend is one who accepts us as we are — when we're at our best — or at our worst.

God is such a friend. He sees through the unreal image we sometimes present to others, or even to ourselves.

He accepts us "as is."

He is ready to make His power available.

Once you believe this, you'll feel the comfort of His abiding Love.

◄ ►

You, our God, are kind and true,
patient, and ruling all things in mercy.
For even if we sin we are Yours.
— Wisdom of Solomon 15:1-2

Because you might think your prayer is inadequate doesn't mean you are failing to please God.

Most people expect too much of themselves. Everyone has difficulty with prayer. We human beings are so easily discouraged. When we allow this to happen, we are being unkind to ourselves. And our prayer becomes less supportive than God intends it to be.

God wants us to feel confident about His love, for His love is eternal and unfailing.

The Lord is kind and tender with us. Can we dare to be anything but kind and tender with ourselves as we travel our inner journey?

Be at peace then. Good feelings are not necessary in that love relationship called prayer.

God's Love transcends all.

◀ ▶

> *As the Lord has forgiven you,*
> *so you also must forgive.*
> *— Colossians 3:13*

What is forgiveness?

Derived from the Old English "forgiefan," to forgive, it is defined as "to give up resentment; to cease to feel resentment against on account of a wrong committed." In German, the verb is "vergeben," meaning to give over or to grant.

To say "I forgive you" is to free yourself from the shackles of holding some grudge that weighs on the mind and burdens the soul.

Telling someone you forgive them does not condone the wrong, it merely means you have decided to give up stewing about it, especially if the person is sorry.

Look to Christ, who is the expert on forgiveness. Pray for the necessary strength and patience to imitate Him.

◀ ▶

You have turned my mourning into dancing;
You have taken off my sackcloth and clothed me
with joy, so that my soul may praise You and
not be silent. O Lord my God, I will
give You thanks forever.
— Psalm 30:11-12

"I had been going through a very difficult time eight years ago.

"My father had terminal cancer, causing my mother to move in with me after suffering a second stroke. My marriage of fifteen years was in trouble. I had four dependent children.

"I was smoking two and a half packs of cigarettes a day, and I was beginning to drink at night before going to sleep so that I wouldn't have to lie there thinking about the pain that was waiting for me the following morning.

"I ran into a friend whom I hadn't seen in a long time. She told me about this New Life she had found in Jesus, and asked me to join her for a Christian women's luncheon. I don't remember the name of the minister, but I will never forget his subject: Jesus Christ and His message of God's love.

"I have fallen in love with Jesus Christ and His Gospel, and can truly say that He is the Rock I now build my life upon."

— D.R., Stratford, CT

◄ ►

*The one who sows sparingly will also reap
sparingly, and the one who sows bountifully
will also reap bountifully. Each of you must
give as you have made up your mind, not
reluctantly or under compulsion,
for God loves a cheerful giver.*
— 2 Corinthians 9:6-7

People are drawn to the performing arts for all
kinds of reasons. Some are attracted by fame or
by riches but there are also those who simply love
to give pleasure to others.

The desire to give of ourselves is the noblest
motive that one can have in any profession.

Throughout history, God has showered His gifts
lavishly upon us. He gives us the gift of love, the
gift of life, and for those who have ears, the gift
of wisdom.

In the fullness of time, God even shared Himself by giving us the gift of His only begotten Son,
Jesus Christ.

In return, God asks us to give generously of
our own talents and gifts.

We imitate God's goodness every time we respond to the needs of others.

◄ ►

I call upon God;
and the Lord will save me.
Morning, noon and night
I utter my complaint and moan,
and He will hear my voice.
— Psalm 55:16-17

If spirituality means responding to God from moment to moment, then it is also a uniquely personal experience.

The spiritual life of a person can never be exactly duplicated. You cannot copy someone else. You can only live your own unique personal life with God.

You can admire the great spiritual leaders, but you shouldn't presume that the Lord is leading you in exactly the same way He led them. You are different. You are beautiful in your own distinctive way.

Try not to copy anyone. A copy is a counterfeit. It means losing freshness, originality and spontaneity. You must be yourself.

Moan, cry, laugh, and sing your own song.

◄ ►

May 1

There is . . . no gladness above joy of heart.
— *Sirach 30:16*

Christ's message is one of joy and hope. He never intended us to be somber and morose in our pursuit of His will.

Laughter is a gift — one that you must first accept and cultivate within yourself before you can share it with others. You need not be a stand-up comedian to have a sense of humor, either. Developing a sense of humor begins with adjusting the way you see yourself.

Extracting the humor from your own mistakes, idiosyncrasies, and faults builds the foundation for a healthy outlook toward yourself and the world around you. Once you learn to take yourself less seriously, chances are you'll become more tolerant of the imperfections in others.

The person with a sense of humor shares jokes, anecdotes, or something cheerful with another, spreading the gift of laughter.

The person with a sense of humor will also recognize the comic side of the hassles and situations we encounter every day.

Choose laughter over irritation, you'll feel better, and so will those around you.

◀ ▶

Everyone is searching for You.
— *Mark 1:37*

"A few years ago, I felt a constant uneasiness. It was as if someone was trying to speak but I couldn't hear over the louder noises and stresses in my life.

"After many months of feeling 'what is it?' clearly, with an indescribable tenderness and passion, I heard, 'I love you.'

"It has taken me a long time to accept this gift. My life has never been the same.

"Three years later, my uneasiness sent me out on one of my innumerable searches for a perfect church where I would fit. I found myself at the door of the Catholic Church in my own neighborhood. Could it be this simple? Since then, my husband and I have renewed our marriage vows in the church, our children have been baptized and my eldest son has received his First Communion.

"I haven't stopped my searching, but the search has become a joy. God has made a promise to me — 'You haven't seen anything yet!'"

— A.F., Hyattsville, MD

◀ ▶

I do not call you servants any longer . . .
I have called you friends.
— John 15:15

During His time on earth, Jesus enjoyed the companionship of both men and women. Peter and John, Mary, Martha, and Lazarus were some of them.

For these people, Jesus was not only a savior. He was a loyal friend.

Do you ever think of Jesus as your friend? As someone who is interested in your happiness?

Jesus knows how easily we are discouraged . . . how many mistakes we make. He knows how much we need forgiveness, comfort, and courage. Because of this He constantly offers His loving support.

Let the Lord be your Best Friend.

◀ ▶

*The Lord passed by, and a great
and strong wind rent the mountains . . .
and after the wind an earthquake . . .
and after the earthquake a fire . . .
and after the fire a still small voice.
And when Elijah heard it,
he wrapped his face in his mantle.*
— *1 Kings 19:11,12-13*

Sometimes it takes a great disaster to wake us up to God's presence within us.

And we can gain some perspective on our own prayer life by observing Elijah. We are, after all, like him, only human.

Listening for that still, small voice, which is the voice of God, requires effort.

Many have enjoyed God's presence, and have listened for His voice. They do not know how to put into words what they experience because the experience is indescribable.

It doesn't matter. All one has to do is honor God by believing in His love and His union with your inmost being.

Enjoy His company throughout the day. And from time to time listen for His voice.

◀ ▶

God called the dry land Earth, and
the waters that were gathered together
He called Seas.
And God saw that it was good.
— Genesis 1:10

"Love all God's creation, the whole and every grain of sand in it.

"Love every leaf, every ray of God's light.

"Love the animals, love the plants, love everything.

"If you love everything, you will perceive the divine mystery in things.

"Once you perceive it, you will begin to comprehend it better every day.

"And you will come at last to love the whole world with an all-embracing love."

Feodor Dostoevski

◀ ▶

To the Lord our God belong
mercy and forgiveness.
— Daniel 9:9

"I believe Jesus is the Son of God. Through Him it is possible to gain eternal life. At the same time, the closer you try to follow Him, the tougher it gets.

"As soon as you feel you have no serious sins, you look deeper inside and find many areas that need improvement. In seeking reconciliation, too many of the same things keep coming up. The good news is the great feeling of forgiveness.

"You feel good getting up for early Mass each day. You give thanks for all that has been given to us, prayers for family, friends, and the lonely, the sick, those in prison, and less fortunate. You ask for help during the day.

"I know He is always with me. I don't know why I don't always recognize Him."

— T.B., Logansport, IN

◀ ▶

May 7

*Put away from you all bitterness and wrath
and anger and wrangling and slander,
together with all malice,
and be kind to one another,
tenderhearted, forgiving one another,
as God in Christ has forgiven you.*
— Ephesians 4:31-32

Shakespeare wrote that the quality of mercy is twice blessed — it blesses those who give and those who receive.

We know mercy and forgiveness aren't always easy and yet without a spirit of forgiveness, life can be miserable.

Forgiveness can be difficult, especially if we've been wounded deeply. But, as one observer has noted, forgiveness isn't much of a virtue unless it involves striving to pardon what we may feel is unpardonable.

The personal benefits of forgiveness are many. It can free us from resentment, it can heal a broken relationship.

Forgiveness heals at least two people: the one who forgives as well as the one in need of forgiveness.

◄ ►

Do not grow weary when you pray.
— Sirach 7:10

An elderly Religious Sister describes her prayer life over the years:

"All that I can offer God now is myself, my tiny bit of physical work and pain, plus the longing to continue to be of use to all.

"Please understand, I am an old lady trying to be ever closer to my Divine Spouse and yet, and here is the paradox, very worldly in thoughts and acts.

"How do I pray? At one time I thought I was praying only when I was able to kneel before our Lord in the Blessed Sacrament.

"Then came the realization that teaching was prayer.

"But now there is dryness, aridity and very seldom 'sweetness.' All that I can manage is 'Praise Jesus!' or 'Come, O Holy Spirit' — a few short prayers. And trying to find Him in the other Sisters and older people here."

◄ ►

Encourage one another and
build one another up.
— 1 Thessalonians 5:11

How often have you felt discouraged, and all it took to get your motivation in gear was the enthusiastic encouragement of a friend? When you encourage others, you build them up.

Sometimes people become discouraged simply because they lack the support of family and friends. By telling them, "you can do it" or "I give you credit for trying so hard, don't give up," you fuel their perseverance and help them fulfill their potential.

Encouragement is a welcome display of support and love that says, "I believe in you!"

Children have a special need for encouragement. Parents can express support by assisting with homework or offering a ride to some after-school activity. Every task a child undertakes gives parents an opportunity to offer encouragement.

◄ ►

> *The Lord is my strength and my shield;*
> *in Him my heart trusts.*
> — *Psalm 28:7*

"As a little girl growing up, I would dream that one day a knight in shining armor would come and rescue me from all the loneliness, sadness and injustices that surrounded me.

"I am now a grown woman and no longer have that dream because our Lord, Jesus Christ has rescued me.

"Jesus Christ is my knight in shining armor. I call when I am in distress. He protects me. I am lost. He finds me. I am lonely, He fills me with His presence. I am empty and He sets my heart aglow with His love, without asking and in abundance.

"He asked me to accept His love for me so that I may be able to pass it on to others. Compassion, kindness, patience and forgiveness given freely and unconditionally out of His love; to me, through me to others. Just small acts of mercy performed sometimes out of mutual love. Would I do this for Him? How could I say no?

"I love Him."

— L.M., Chatham, NJ

◀ ▶

May 11

Blessed are you when people revile you and persecute you and utter all kinds of evil against you falsely on My account. Rejoice and be glad, for your reward is great in heaven, for in the same way they persecuted the prophets who were before you.
— *Matthew 5:11*

Sometimes people ridicule us when we go out on a limb for God. Jesus knew that would happen.

It may seem contradictory to speak of happiness in the same breath as risk-taking and persecution, but countless saints testify to the fact that when they were faithful to the Lord in difficult circumstances, they experienced the deepest joy they had ever known.

The gift of joy is beyond our natural understanding, but it grows and grows in proportion to our trust.

Jesus assured us that once we truly believe in God's saving love, and act on our belief that He is truly with us at all times, the miseries of this life would no longer disturb us. It is in times of trial that He wants us to remember His love.

Trials, therefore, are actually opportunities for spiritual growth. If we see the cross only as a burden, we miss a wonderful chance to grow and to delight the Lord with our trust.

◄ ►

Pray to the Most High continually.
— 2 Esdras 9:25

Another religious sister reflected on how she prays:

"There are times when, for me, praying is just *listening*. My most intense prayers are 'said' in this manner. Before the Eucharistic presence, listening becomes a person-to-person conversation."

Then there is the prayer of *talking to God:*

"When I have an opportunity to be outdoors, the beauty of nature, in whatever form it might be — clouds, trees, earth — makes me conscious of the God above and His loving concern for me. I love it . . . You don't do things in a small way, your love is limitless.

"Finally, I have prayer books, too, from which I *pray* my prayers. This gives a certain type of discipline to my life, from which I enjoy inner peace."

Blessed are those who hear.
— Revelation 1:3

"Prayer without listening, is like picking up the telephone, dialing God, and saying, 'Hey God, I have this problem' and then hanging up without even waiting for an answer," said Susan Dobson, an entertainment producer and business manager.

"Now I slow down and sit still and go to my house of prayer within."

God speaks to us in many ways. We have to slow down to listen.

Trappist monk Father Thomas Keating says, "God's first language is silence and everything else is translation."

And so "when one allows oneself to be really still, beyond thinking," that allows us to grasp "an intuitive sense of a deeper Presence than ourselves."

It's possible to listen to God with our heart; to listen in the sights, sounds and beauty of the natural world.

Learn to listen.

◀ ▶

> *Look, on the mountains,*
> *the feet of one*
> *who brings good tidings,*
> *who proclaims peace.*
> — *Nahum 1:15*

"I am in good company at the feet of Jesus. He has given me His own Mother, the Queen of Heaven, and His brothers and sisters.

"And yet I still foolishly wander from the Cross of Life. On my return, He lifts me up and holds me to His wounded heart that never stops loving me. 'I am going to the Father to prepare a place for you.'

"'Lord, I am not worthy,' I cry.

"He teaches me the power of prayer. To pray is to love. 'Let everything you do, each person you touch by thought or word or deed, every breath in you, be wrapped in prayer. When I return to take you with me, bring along all that you have ever loved, and offer it to the Father, the source of eternal life.'"

— A.V., South Africa

◀ ▶

> *Blessed are the meek*
> *for they shall inherit the earth.*
> — *Matthew 5:5*

During His earthly life, Jesus encountered many people who suffered from illnesses, both physical and psychological. To each of them He brought not only healing, but the Good News of their infinite worth and dignity in the sight of God.

As His ministry reached its fulfillment on the cross, Jesus made His identification with the weak and suffering of this world complete.

Through the cross, He asks His followers in every generation to recognize Him in all those who suffer and who carry heavy psychological burdens and difficulties.

So look for opportunities to help and comfort those around you. By drawing close to them in their need, you'll be drawing close to the Lord.

◄ ►

*We went through fire and water; yet You, (God)
have brought us out to a spacious place.*
— *Psalm 66:12*

The great paintings of Rembrandt are charac-
terized by the artist's genius in capturing the play
of light. His figures seem to emerge from darkness
into a cascade of golden brilliance. But to attain
this effect, Rembrandt had to spend considerable
time mixing dark colors to create the shadows.

If you had come upon him working, you might
have thought he was trying to produce a sad and
gloomy work. But no. With a little patience you
would have realized that the dark colors show off
the golden light in its best setting.

The Lord of Life is the greatest artist and we
are His masterpieces. Each of us is a work in progress, a masterpiece in the making. There are times
in our life when we are lost in the shadows. Moods
are dark. The world seems hostile. Our best efforts
fail. We are full of fear and doubt.

But things are never as bleak as they seem. We
see only the shadows. God sees the finished
masterpiece of our lives.

◄ ►

> *Be angry but do not sin;*
> *do not let the sun go down*
> *on your anger.*
> *— Ephesians 4:26*

Anger is a complex emotion. Anger used to defeat another person is destructive, but anger which leads to forgiveness is a valuable and constructive emotion.

We get angry at ourselves for the things we do — or fail to do. We get angry at others for hurts or perceived slights, whether they're real or even intended. We get angry at misfortune and sometimes we rail at God like Job did.

Anger is a part of our lives, but we can't allow it to turn to bitterness, resentment, or hatred — these things are not from God.

Bitter people hold on to their anger until it sours their spirit. Hurt may grip the spirit for a time, but those who call upon God's grace are delivered from bitterness through forgiveness.

Keep in mind that even if you're filled with bad feelings toward someone you still have the power to forgive.

Do not let the sun go down on your anger.

◄ ►

"As a teenager, I felt defeated and was very troubled. My parents had divorced when I was very young. My mother married an Army officer a few years later. We toured the world, but I felt an emptiness in my life.

"In 1969, I found myself in a combat role in Vietnam. My unit was stationed about 17 miles north of Saigon. We were attacked by mortars and rockets every night. I was terrified by the constant explosions and utter despair.

"I stumbled inside the base chapel one evening and heard the chaplain preach on the text:

"For God so loved the world that He gave His only Son that whoever believes in Him should not perish but have eternal life. (John 3:16)

"I felt God speaking directly to me.

"Today, I am a member of a Baptist church. I have a wonderful Christian wife, two wonderful boys, aged five and 10. We are blessed today because of Him. Praise God!"

— C.V., Acworth, GA

◄ ►

> *Come to Me, all you that are weary*
> *and are carrying heavy burdens,*
> *and I will give you rest.*
> *— Matthew 11:28*

Each person has a part to play in making this a better world. And each day offers opportunities to integrate spiritual values into your life, whether it's on the job, in school or in the home.

Each one of us can be a positive influence on those closest to us.

We can also influence politicians, business leaders, and professionals by letting them know the values we hold dear, and by encouraging them to live up to the highest ideals of the human spirit.

You may want to choose a career where you will have a direct impact on the way others think and act.

Or, maybe you're already in the hardest and most influential job of all — parenting.

No matter what it is you do in life, your personal touch is important. Give the best you can to your calling in life.

◄ ►

I am my beloved's and my beloved is mine.
— Song of Solomon 6:3

"All my life I have prayed: the simple prayers of childhood; the desperate prayers of fear and sorrow, the mechanical reciting of the daily rosary for thirty-four years.

"Ten to fifteen years ago I ventured into forms of meditation, or active contemplation.

"Since then, I can only say I believe God has led me along the path of pure contemplation, or mystical prayer.

"I feel God's presence continually. My love for Him is increasing. My faith and hope grow. My awareness of my sins intensifies without becoming overwhelming. My attachments fade. And, I am starting to know what the words 'joy' and 'peace' mean.

"The only prayer that I seem able to put into words is: God's will be done.

"He leads me to union with Him so that He can live in me."

— Anon.

◄ ►

> *What good is it, my brothers and sisters,*
> *if you say you have faith*
> *but do not have works?*
> — *James 2:14*

First comes faith, then love, and then dedicated service. To say that anyone is a "dedicated person" is high tribute, especially if his or her devotion promotes the common good.

Such a person is in striking contrast to those who are so self-centered that they never give of themselves to family, friends or fellow workers, much less to the big issues that are convulsing the world.

The word "dedicated" comes from the Latin "dedicatus sum" meaning "I have given myself."

You are only one. But you are one. You can't do everything but you can do something and what you can do you should try to do.

Dedicate yourself for love of God to the task of making this a better world and your whole life will take on a fuller meaning.

◄ ►

I walked in the ways of truth.
— *Tobit 1:3*

"Jesus is Number One in my life, my personal Lord and Savior. He is in me and I in Him. He is the most constant and faithful being in my life — my hope in the present, and my hope in the future. His saving grace is always with me, resurrecting and healing me.

"When I wander away from Him, He is there patiently waiting to take me back unconditionally. My struggling to remain Christlike in the world is a lifelong one — knowing that I will be judged on ordinary, everyday living.

"With my free acceptance of Jesus' Spirit within me, I become the living Christ: *It is no longer I who live, but it is Christ Who lives in Me.* (Galatians 2:20)

"Because of His presence in my life, my journey here on earth is made easier and more bearable. As I give myself to Jesus, I also give myself to humanity. We are the body of Christ!"
— H.P., Cresskill, NJ

◀ ▶

> *See what love the Father has given us,*
> *that we should be called children of*
> *God, and that is what we are.*
> *— 1 John 3:1*

A parent will always accept the imperfections of his or her own children. This simple comparison helps us to see ourselves from God's perspective.

We are sometimes told how we can offend God, but little is ever said of the incredible power we have to please Him. How a human being, a struggling sinner at that, can please the Lord is the most fascinating part of religion.

We were made for happiness because we are made in the image of Happiness personified. The very thought of a future united with the source of all joy brings pleasure to the soul.

If you have the eyes to see, and the faith to understand, you will see that you are a precious child of God. The spirit of Jesus is living in you. You have by Baptism become the hand and the voice of Christ in your particular sphere of influence.

All of God's children who open themselves to the indwelling Spirit become instruments of God's love in this world.

◀ ▶

Jesus, the Christ, laid down a condition for prayer to be effective:

> *If you forgive others their trespasses,*
> *your heavenly Father will also forgive you;*
> *but if you do not forgive others,*
> *neither will your Father forgive your trespasses.*
> (Matthew 6:14-15)

These words are to be taken seriously.

We all tend to grumble and complain more than we should. We need to be more charitable, more than we are.

It is rare when a person is being criticized to hear someone else speak up in his or her defense. Not merely forgiving them, but reminding others of their good qualities, this is rare indeed.

Try to be more understanding. More forgiving. Do unto others as you would have them do unto you.

◄ ►

Come, let us walk in the light of the Lord.
— Isaiah 2:5

"No heaven can come to us unless our hearts find rest in today. Take heaven!

"No peace lies in the future which is not hidden in this present instant. Take peace!

"The gloom of the world is but a shadow. Behind it, yet within reach is joy.

"There is radiance and glory in the darkness could we but see. And to see we have only to look. I beseech you to look.

"Life is so generous a giver, but we, judging its gifts by their covering, cast them away as ugly, or heavy, or hard.

"Remove the covering and you find beneath it a living splendor, woven of love by wisdom, with power . . ."

— Fra Giovanni

If we remain in the shadows of anxiety or sorrow, we cannot see the light of God's love and peace. But it is all around us. We have only to trust God and take the step in the dark that brings us back into the sunlight.

◄ ►

*Ask the plants of the earth, and they will teach
you ... Who among you does not know that
the hand of the Lord has done this?*
— *Job 12:8,9*

"It was a warm spring day. The kind when one
can feel, smell and hear a new season revealing
itself. Any change in season is not without its
chores. My chore that breezy afternoon was to
till the garden.

"My mind wandered back to conversations with
several coworkers. They confessed to having a personal relationship with Jesus, an idea I scoffed
at, yet I became more curious about. There was
a sincerity, a genuineness and a peace about them.
I secretly yearned for whatever it was that they
possessed.

"I was surprised to find myself praying for a
change in my life. Suddenly, something mysterious
started happening.

"That very instant, I gave my life over to Jesus.
I confessed to Him that I was a sinner and wished
to sin no longer. I placed my life in His hands.

"Because of His love for me, He has trans-
formed my life from one of bondage to one of
freedom. Freedom to live my life as His ambas-
sador glorifying Him in all I do."

— L.D., Newton, NJ

◄ ►

> *I hereby command you:*
> *Be strong and courageous;*
> *do not be frightened or dismayed,*
> *for the Lord your God is*
> *with you wherever you go.*
> *— Joshua 1:9*

Community life has the best chance of thriving in those cities and towns where residents get personally involved; where they feel individually responsible for one another.

When people fail to get involved, it's often because of fear and not apathy. That's an understandable reaction. They want to help out, but given modern realities, they're afraid. But we should never allow fear to cripple us.

Pray for courage. When you call upon the Lord to be your strength, you can overcome your fears.

Don't be afraid to be a vital part of your community. Neighbors have to work together in order to create communities which are safe for young and old.

◀ ▶

> *Trust in the Lord with all your heart*
> *and do not rely on your own insight.*
> — *Proverbs 3:5*

Trust is at the basis of true dependence on the Lord. But how do you achieve the state of total dependence on God? You don't achieve it. You accept it as a gift.

The realization of our utter dependence on God dawns on us only imperceptibly over a long period of time. It is a gift that God reveals ever so slowly.

We can desire it.

We can pray for the grace to grow more trusting and more dependent on the Lord.

We can ask ourselves whether we believe that the Father's will for us coincides with our peace and happiness. For the truth is that in His will we find our peace.

Our challenge is to allow the Lord to lead us.

◄ ►

> *May the Lord give strength*
> *to His people!*
> *May the Lord bless*
> *His people with peace!*
> *— Psalm 29:11*

Inspire us, O God, with such a deep love of country that we will be as actively concerned for its welfare as for that of all our fellow citizens.

Teach us to show by word and deed zealous interest in protecting and furthering the spiritual principles upon which our nation was founded.

Teach us likewise to share with every one of Your children the same love, peace, and joy You have given to us.

Amen.

◀ ▶

May 30

> *Let us crown ourselves*
> *with rosebuds*
> *before they wither.*
> — *Wisdom of Solomon 2:8*

"I send this poem to you to explain who Jesus is to me.

"I am not worried about my arthritis pain. To me, it is like this haiku I composed:

"Smelling the sweet rose
My temple presses a thorn
Still the scent lingers."

— I.W., Lexington, MA

◄ ►

The wisdom from above is first pure,
then peaceable, gentle, willing to yield,
full of mercy and good fruits,
without a trace of partiality or hypocrisy.
— James 3:17

The word *mercy* means to show compassion toward an offender or an enemy.

During his time on earth, Jesus taught us, both in words and in action, how to show mercy to those around us.

In the Gospel of John, we are told the story of Christ's encounter with a woman about to be stoned for adultery. Rather than condemning her, He came to her defense.

Jesus condemned sin but never the sinner. His mercy is boundless and limitless.

And we are called to live our lives the same way.

◄ ►

June 1

The one who keeps the Law makes many offerings; one who heeds the commandments makes an offering of well-being ... to forsake unrighteousness is an atonement.
— *Sirach 35:1-2,5*

Prayer produces a sweet spirit. A sweet spirit is filled with charity, patience and kindness toward others, toward self. You cannot be kind to others if you cannot be kind to yourself.

Bitterness is the enemy of sweetness of spirit. How many bitter people have you met who try to have an active prayer life? They may say prayers, but bitterness and resentment fill their hearts.

The longer you nurse your bitterness, the longer you postpone your liberation.

Pray for the gift of a loving heart. And free yourself from bitterness of spirit.

◀ ▶

God's love has been poured into
our hearts through the Holy Spirit that
has been given to us.
— Romans 5:5

"To live a prayerful life we cannot do without specific prayers. We need to say them in such a way that we can listen better to the Spirit praying in us. We need to continue to include all people . . .

"Through our prayers we can carry in our heart all human pain and sorrow, all conflicts and agonies, all torture and war, all hunger, loneliness, and misery, not because of some great psychological or emotional capacity, but because God's heart has become one with ours."

— Henri Nouwen, "The Way of the Heart"

◄ ►

I have sinned by betraying innocent blood.
— *Matthew 27:4*

"Five years ago, my very dear friend, whom I had helped in countless ways, betrayed me. For three weeks I shed a thousand tears. I forgave this person and prayed the Prayer of St. Francis dozens of times a day. Still it came back to my mind day and night.

"One morning before Mass I asked the Lord this: 'You know my hurt feelings and you know I forgave this person, so please heal me so I can forget it.'

"Right after the consecration at Mass I felt an unusual warmth around my heart and I thought something was happening to me. Then I heard the Lord speak clearly and this is what He said, 'I have seen your tears. I was betrayed by a friend, too. Since you are following me, you have to expect adversity. But if you stay close to me I'll be your friend. I will never betray you. I will never reject you. I love you.'

"With that He lifted my burden and filled me with inexpressible joy. My faith was always strong but now I not only believe in God but I know He lives."

— A.E., Waite Park, MN

◄ ►

May prayer be made for Him
continually, and blessings invoked
for Him all day long.
— Psalm 72:15

Praying to the Father is a private matter.

The Lord's love is personal. When you address Him, do it for His eyes only.

When you go about doing good in the world, keep the same attitude in mind. He is very much aware of your noble intentions and desires. His affection for you is a given fact. Have no doubt about it.

Your task is to be open to His love.

Playing to the crowd is insincere, immature, and disrespectful.

There are countless opportunities to be personal with the Lord. All it takes is a little imagination.

◀ ▶

June 5

Turn to the Lord and forsake your sins;
pray in His presence.
— Sirach 17:25

Your prayer is your life with God. The prayer you offer at any given moment arises from your heart.

You have to find the way of lifting your mind and heart to God that best suits you.

Give yourself to God in your own words. It really is simple and uncomplicated.

God is always present. His love is infinite and unchanging.

Remind yourself of God's love, and take the time to be with Him in your own way every day.

◄ ►

June 6

O Lord, Your steadfast love
is better than life.
— Psalm 63:3

If you don't feel God's love, there's no need to be discouraged.

Think of a cloudy day. You may not feel the sun's warmth on a cloudy day, but you know it's there.

God's love is like the sun. It is always there whether you feel it or not.

At times you may feel God has abandoned you but His love is as constant and unchanging as the sun.

◀ ▶

June 7

The Spirit of the Lord will carry you
I know not where.
— 1 Kings 18:12

"Four years ago my husband died of cancer and I was totally lost. I had no desire to live and prayed every night for God to take me, too.

"I got on my knees in front of the Sacred Heart and cried like a newborn baby. I begged God to take me, use me, make me, mold me, do anything necessary to give me peace.

"All of a sudden I didn't have a care in the world. It was like ten tons had been lifted off my shoulders.

"The minute I open my eyes in the morning, I ask Jesus to purify me from head to toe, and I ask the Holy Spirit to guide and teach me and help me plant at least one seed to help somebody daily. I don't care how tired I am or how bad I feel, I can't wait to see what the Holy Spirit is going to do with me.

"There is nothing in this world that God can't take care of."

— J.C., Freeport, TX

◀ ▶

Take delight in the Lord,
and He will give you
the desires of your heart.
— Psalm 37:4

All holy desires are a gift from God.

St. Augustine wrote: "The entire life of a good Christian is in fact an exercise of holy desire. You do not yet see what you long for, but the very act of desiring prepares you so that when He comes, you may see and be utterly satisfied."

What does St. Augustine mean by the phrase, "the very act of desiring prepares you"? I think his words can be taken on face value. For instance, when you smell food cooking, your appetite comes alive. You want to sample the delicious treat being conjured up before your eyes. In the same way, God prepares your heart for the great encounter that will take place in Heaven.

As you develop a taste for God, and allow it to grow into a flaming desire, your soul will expand and magnify your love. God will lead you to new heights precisely through the desires of your heart.

◄ ►

> *O God, You are my God,*
> *I seek You, my soul thirsts for You;*
> *my flesh faints for You,*
> *as in a dry and weary land*
> *where there is no water.*
> *— Psalm 63:1*

Prayer is not so much a matter of mastering a technique and persevering in it. Rather, prayer is simply communicating with God.

One approach worth cultivating is the ancient Jesus Prayer which is seven words long: "Lord Jesus Christ, have mercy on me."

It is recited throughout the day in the firm belief that Jesus' presence is within; that His very presence brings holiness; that because of His mercy one's own unworthiness counts for nothing.

Eventually quiet prayer will come naturally. Meditation will become easier and more frequent.

The very desire to pray is prayer.

The art of prayer is in enjoying God's continual presence.

◀ ▶

Let us not grow weary in doing what is right,
for we will reap at harvest time,
if we do not give up.
So then, whenever we have an opportunity,
let us work for the good of all.
— Galatians 6:9-10

To give to others is also to give to God.

The opportunities for giving of self through service are endless. You can serve as a volunteer to an established agency, or on a one-to-one basis with a handicapped person, an elderly neighbor, a new mother.

Self-giving also involves fidelity to truth.

There are gifts to be given to individuals and gifts to be given to society. For instance, in overcoming the lie of racism, we stand up for truth although this may not be an easy thing to do.

The key is to always follow the example of Jesus.

◄ ►

From the cloud a voice said,
"This is My beloved Son,
with Him I am well pleased;
listen to Him."
— *Matthew 17:5*

"I believe that Jesus Christ is truly the Son of God. He is our Savior, our Brother, and our Friend. I believe that He is both God and man, an astonishing mystery, which leaves us in deep wonderment. And at the same time it allows us to be strengthened, and to grow closer to Him.

"I believe that Jesus is the Word of God made flesh, that He was destined in time and eternity to be conceived of the Holy Spirit and born of Mary. I believe that Jesus lived on earth in complete obedience to the will of His Father, that God sent Him to show us His love and redemption, and to show us how to live as sons and daughters of God.

"My wonderful wife has been the dynamic source of inspiration in my life. Since we wed, I have gained self-confidence, and have experienced untold joy and happiness. I believe that Jesus Christ has brought us happily together. Jesus, by His word and presence is joy for all ages."

— P.C., East Boston, MA

◀ ▶

Whatever you ask for in prayer,
believe that you have received it,
and it will be yours.
— Mark 11:24

Prayer is the expression of our desire.

Prayer is the outpouring of our faith.

God is pleased with an authentic faith which is free of doubt. His love is unchanging and unconditional. That means a believer can have certainty about it. But this is not a wide-eyed belief in some vague divine insurance policy. Christian faith is firm in the knowledge that our relationship with God is personal, and the things Jesus promised are true and "will come to pass."

Jesus is the basis of our faith and He is the reason for our certainty. He is also the object of our faith. Through Him we come to know God, the Father.

Not only does Jesus give us new knowledge about God, He assures us that if we abide in Him, He will empower us to carry His Spirit into the world so that through us wonderful things will begin to happen.

◄ ►

June 13

*Your children, whom You loved, O Lord,
(learned) that it is not the production of crops
that feeds humankind but that Your words
(sustain) those who trust in You.*
— *Wisdom of Solomon 16:26*

Jesus echoed Solomon when He said that people do not live by bread alone.

The Lord has asked us to trust Him with so great a trust that our lives would no longer seem to be our own.

He asks us not to be anxious about tomorrow nor about the future state of our health, or our financial position. This does not mean we shirk our responsibilities. However, it does mean we will be free of needless worry.

If we can free ourselves, if we can believe that the future is in God's hands, we will live in peace.

All we need do is make a sensible effort to trust our loving Lord. He will do the rest.

Ask, and He will give the gift of perfect trust.

◀ ▶

Happy is the nation whose God is the Lord.
— *Psalm 33:12*

A belief in God has been a hallmark of American life. Every president without exception has made reference to it. Officeholders, witnesses and jurors all swear an oath before God.

Mention is made of the Creator in the Declaration of Independence. The Pledge of Allegiance to the Flag recognizes the existence of God and our coins proclaim "In God We Trust."

America's founders thought it important to call upon the Deity. In 1787, when the Constitutional Convention ran into difficulties, Benjamin Franklin successfully proposed that each day's deliberations begin with prayer. He said:

"The small progress we have made . . . is, methinks, a melancholy proof of the imperfections of the human understanding . . . I have lived, Sir, a long time; and the longer I live the more convincing proofs I see of this truth, that God governs in the affairs of men.

"And if a sparrow cannot fall to the ground without His notice, is it probable that an empire can rise without His aid?"

◄ ►

June 15

In Your presence is fullness of joy;
in Your right hand are pleasures forevermore.
— Psalm 16:11

"A favorite prayer of mine begins, 'In every need let me come to You with humble trust, saying, "Jesus, help me!"' Another prayer I say daily to Mary ends, 'May I sense the presence of your Divine Son in every second, every minute, and every hour of this day.' These two prayers sum up my relationship with Jesus.

"Besides the obvious sense of gratitude for what Jesus has done by dying for all of us, when I think of Jesus, it's seldom with the awe of approaching God, I feel as though I am contacting a friend — a best friend. He's there when I need to complain. He's there when I have a favor to ask. He's always there. No appointment needed. At times, just thinking about Him brings a lump to my throat and tears to my eyes. I can't imagine a world without Him."

— A.S., DeMotte, IN

◀ ▶

In His final discourse, Jesus explained His purpose on earth: to give glory to the Father, and to give eternal life to those the Father entrusted to Him:

Father, the hour has come: glorify Your Son,
so that Your Son may glorify You, since You
have given Him authority over all people,
to give eternal life to all whom You have
given Him. And this is eternal life,
that they may know You, the only true God,
and Jesus Christ whom You have sent.
I glorified You on earth by finishing
the work You gave Me to do.
(John 17:1-4)

God's love always seeks the good of the person loved, and He rejoices in that good. The love of God is an unselfish love. He does not seek our love for His own advantage. Christ's sacrificial death taught us that God willingly surrenders self-interest to help us. He is always there for us, working little miracles to help us cope.

His love is universal. It extends even to the wicked. Even if we are not able to love our enemies, at least we can try. No one is outside of God's embrace.

◄ ►

> *You show me the path of life.*
> *In Your presence,*
> *there is fullness of joy;*
> *in Your right hand are*
> *pleasures forevermore.*
> *— Psalm 16:11*

Journeys, by definition, involve passage from one place to another.

They can be exciting, but also frightening. It takes a lot of courage to leave behind the familiar and become a stranger in a strange land. Those bold enough to travel to exotic places are often motivated by the love of adventure and the love of freedom.

In a sense, we're all travelers because life itself is a journey. It has a starting point and it has a final destination. And it's important to know who you are and where you're going.

You are a child of God and with His help your life's journey will end in Heaven.

◄ ►

> *(Jesus) took a loaf of bread,*
> *and when He had given thanks,*
> *He broke it and gave it to them, saying,*
> *"This is My Body, which is given for you.*
> *Do this in remembrance of Me."*
> — *Luke 22:19*

Throughout the two thousand years of Christianity, Catholics have depended for their strength and sustenance on Christ in the Eucharist.

In the liturgy only one voice prays, that of the Mystical Body of Jesus Christ offering Himself to the Father. All those attending Mass unite in Him and through Him and with Him in His eternal act of self-oblation.

The Mass is the representation of Christ's death on the cross in ritual form. The body and blood of Christ are truly present under the appearance of bread and wine.

Catholics celebrate Christ's redemptive sacrifice by entering into His surrender to God the Father. The miracle of Christ's coming in the Eucharist is His way of feeding His lambs and His sheep.

◄ ►

June 19

The wind blows where it chooses,
and you hear the sound of it,
but you do not know where it comes from
or where it goes.
— John 4:8

"The Lord is a relentless lover. If we leave even the tiniest crack of the door open, the Lord will push it open wide.

"And in our fright or ignorance or through our wrong, if we push the Lord out again and bolt the door shut, the Lord climbs in a window.

"And if we slam down the window and lock it tight, the Lord stands outside, looking in, waiting patiently for an invitation.

"And if, because of our own sinfulness, we cannot bear to look on the face of the Lord and draw the curtains closed, the Lord will enter through the cracks of our house, on the voice of the wind."

— C.C., Lake Hiawatha, NJ

◄ ►

*You shall love the Lord your God with
all your heart, and with all your soul,
and with all your might.*
— *Deuteronomy 6:5*

God has often been misunderstood. In Medieval spiritual literature there was a strong emphasis on suffering and punishment. That is a truncated understanding of divine revelation.

God is love and love is only interested in the good of the beloved. Love is patient, kind and humble. The Lord came on the earth not to condemn us but to bring us joy.

Jesus died that we might live. He allowed Himself to be devoured by the Living God so that the whole human race would be freed to receive His eternal glory.

The notion of sacrificial love is more understandable when we reduce it to life-size proportions. For instance, a mother who gives up her sleep to care for a sick child is rewarded when the child gets well. Even if the child never says, "Thank you," her joy comes in the loving.

God's love is like that. He doesn't count the cost, nor does He ask for your permission to care for you. He simply loves because He is Love.

◀ ▶

> *Pray to your Father.*
> — *Matthew 6:6*

"*Our Father,* heavenly Father, how great is Your Name!

"*Thy kingdom come,* You sent us Your Son as our means of salvation.

"*Thy will be done on earth as it is in heaven.* Father, You said, *This is My beloved Son; listen to Him.* I listen to His words and accept all His teachings and His will in my life.

"*Give us this day* the Bread of Life which is Your beloved Son, Jesus.

"*Forgive us our trespasses.*

"*And deliver us from all evil.* Guide and protect us. Love us always so that we may always love You. Amen."

— a Construction Worker

◄ ►

> *Parents, do not provoke your children,*
> *or they may lose heart.*
> — *Colossians 3:21*

"Oh Lord, make me a better parent.

"Teach me to understand my children, to listen patiently to what they say and to answer all their questions kindly.

"Keep me from interrupting them and contradicting them.

"Make me as courteous to them as I would have them be to me.

"Give me the courage to confess my sins against my children and to ask their forgiveness when I know I have done them wrong . . .

"Help me to grow with my children, to treat them as those of their own age; but let me not expect of them the judgments and conventions of adults.

"Allow me not to rob them of the opportunity to wait upon themselves, to think, to choose, and to make decisions."

— Cary C. Myers, "The Modern Parent"

◀ ▶

"Jesus not only loves me unconditionally but He trusts me with His power. No matter how challenging or frightening the task confronting me, He will join with me to surmount it. Yet I often forget to ask, to trust, and I get into a big muddle or mess. Through gritted teeth, in frustration and anger, I cry out, 'Jesus, help me!'

"If only I remember to pray beforehand, 'Jesus, I can't handle this alone, please be with me,' or, 'Jesus, I'm afraid, I'm lonely, I'm weak and cannot resist temptation, I'm tired and can't go on, help me, Jesus.' How easily it is all settled. Amazing! Amazing Grace?

"Jesus wants me to be happy and to enjoy this beautiful world and the life He has given me. So *go eat your bread with enjoyment, and drink your wine with a merry heart.* (Ecclesiastes 9:7)

"He loves me and lucky me, I know it. The mystery is that I am 74 years old and did not come to this realization until about ten years ago. Through being led to the need we all have for a private prayer time, I gained the knowledge to worry about nothing, instead pray about everything and thank God for His answers. Such freedom!"

— W.O., Streator, IL

◄ ►

I love You, O Lord, my strength.
The Lord is my rock, my fortress
and my deliverer, my God, my rock,
in whom I take refuge, my shield,
and the horn of my salvation, my stronghold.
— Psalm 18:1-2

God our Father wants us to be happy with Him
for all eternity, beginning now.

Therefore, trust your imagination. Visualize the
whole range of gifts God has waiting for you, sur-
prises planned for you from all eternity: the healing of broken relationships; a brand new, healthy
body; peace of soul; and a rich enjoyment of God
Himself. He will bring you the fullness of life
because He loves you and He wants your happiness.

God is a passionate lover.

O gentle Father,
Help me to believe in Your love,
in good times and bad.
Teach me to seek and find You,
that I may love You,
not for what You can do for me,
but for Yourself alone.

◀ ▶

*Beware of practicing your piety before
others . . . Whenever you pray, do not be like the
hypocrites; for they love to . . . be seen by
others . . . do not heap up empty phrases as the
Gentiles do . . . thinking they will be heard
because of their many words.*
— *Matthew 6:1,5,7*

Private prayer should have the love of God as
its primary purpose.

To pray in order to be known as a prayerful person or for any reason other than to ask for forgiveness, to adore God, to thank God or to seek
His favor is to misunderstand the whole meaning of worship.

In prayer we do not have to force feelings of
any kind. We acknowledge Jesus as Lord and we
plead for His healing love. In warning us not to
heap up empty phrases like the Gentiles, Jesus is
condemning mindless, heartless prayers.

The only way to pray well is to pray often.

◄ ►

> *I heard the voice of the Lord saying,*
> *"Whom shall I send?" . . . And I said,*
> *"Here am I; send me!"*
> — *Isaiah 6:8*

Here are some thoughts from Marriage Encounter magazine:

And the Lord said, "Go." and I said, "Who me?" And He said, "Yes, you." And I said, "But I'm not ready yet. And there is company coming. And I can't leave the kids. And You know there's no one to take my place." And He said, "You're stalling."

And the Lord said, "Go." And I said, "But I don't want to." And He said, "I didn't ask if you wanted to." And I said, "Listen, I'm not the kind of person to get involved in controversy. Besides my father won't like it. And what will my neighbors think?" And He said, "Baloney."

And yet a third time the Lord said, "Go."

And I said, "Do I have to?" And He said, "Do you love Me?" And I said, "Look, I'm scared. People are going to hate me. And cut me up in little pieces. I can't take it all by myself." And He said, "Where do you think I'll be?"

And the Lord said, "Go."

And I sighed. "Here I am, send me."

◀ ▶

June 27

Then the hand of the Lord was upon me.
— Ezekiel 3:22

"Alcohol was my answer and end; my God was the Martini. I longed to regain control of my drinking and my life in the worst way, but I couldn't. I was in complete despair and full to the brim with hate toward God, toward my family for not understanding, and mostly, toward myself.

"Three years ago, I awoke one morning and, through blurry eyes, saw my two-year-old son standing beside the bed. I screamed for my husband to take the child away. The emptiness I felt at that moment was complete to the bone. And I could take it no more. I got out of bed, picked up the phone and called for help. A loving friend heard my plea and responded.

"I stopped trying to control everything and did my best at turning the controls over to Jesus. In gentle, subtle ways Jesus is alive in my life, He hugs my soul when I am insecure and reminds me how far I've come. In powerful style, Jesus enables me to write again and has given me a self-confidence about my gift that I never had."

— M.O., Citrus Heights, CA

◄ ►

> *Blessed be God because*
> *He has not rejected my prayer*
> *or removed His steadfast love from me.*
> *— Psalm 66:20*

When it comes to prayer it's important not to force yourself to "feel" a certain way. Don't worry if you can't produce loving or peaceful feelings.

Prayer isn't essentially in emotions. True prayer is in the will to cling to the Lord, regardless of how you feel.

If God doesn't give you the ability to control your emotions, then be content with your imperfect self. This can lead to peace of a more subtle kind.

Remember, God really loves you.

◀ ▶

> *The Lord, our Maker ... is our God,*
> *and we are the people of His pasture,*
> *and the sheep of His hand.*
> *O that today*
> *you would listen to His voice!*
> *— Psalm 95:6,7*

So many people are haunted by past mistakes.

Their suffering in the present, they believe, is directly related to some past error. It hardly ever occurs to them that God's glory will be manifest in His forgiveness and healing.

But Christ assured us of His healing and forgiveness. You have only to desire and seek them. Enjoy His love.

If you are ever going to be happy, let it be today.

◄ ►

Be strong and let your heart take courage.
— Psalm 27:14

Living is a risk. Every undertaking has its uncertainties.

Face the fact that some of your decisions may turn out badly and you'll have to live with it. Or, you may be able to revoke a wrong decision and try again.

But you cannot afford to let fear of the unknown future paralyze you.

"The potential in you is new in nature," said Dr. Ari Kiev of the Cornell Medical Center, "and no one but you can know what you can do, nor will you know until you have tried."

God has entrusted each of us with the challenge to live a life that has never been lived before. How will you use your potential?

Take courage! There is a source of wisdom greater than ourselves. We are not alone, especially at the point of a major decision.

◄ ►

July 1

> *Only You know what is in*
> *every human heart.*
> *— 1 Kings 8:39*

"My early 20's were not smooth years. Inside a tug of war raged about success and failure. I worked at two different careers. Neither one seemed to fit. I felt like a failure. There I was at the age of 26, getting older, no job, no self-esteem.

"I searched for myself in Eastern philosophy, transcendental meditation, EST, Ram Dass and reincarnation . . . I turned to the only source I knew would never reject me. From fall until spring, 1982, I prayed in church for 15 minutes at noon. There I truly poured out my heart and soul to God. I told him of my anguish, my painful memories, my fears. Then one day, Jesus, tender, precious Jesus, said to me, 'I love you.'

"I saw my entire life played out before me. What struck me most was my uniqueness. My individuality. And I saw through the eyes of my Savior His pure joy, His utter delight of me just the way I am!"

— M.T., Cincinnati, OH

◄ ►

> *Those who are wise*
> *shall shine like the brightness of the sky,*
> *and those who lead many*
> *to righteousness,*
> *like the stars forever and ever.*
> — *Daniel 12:3*

If you are truly determined to help others, rather than dominate them, you must be prepared to:

Endure misunderstanding and suffering instead of seeking honor and glory.

Show initiative when most people are apathetic.

Plunge ahead when it would be so easy to drift with the tide.

Take a courageous stand when others are succumbing to expediency or timidity.

Live up to your obligations and responsibilities when there is a strong temptation to neglect or evade them.

If you understand from the very outset that "to lead is to serve" you are bound to accomplish great good in your life.

◀ ▶

Pray to the Most High continually.
— 2 Esdras 9:32

There are some who think of prayer as the rare moment of deep communion with God; as though the day were made up of profane time and sacred time.

Prayer makes time sacred. Continual prayer makes all time sacred. The Jesus Prayer can serve as a prelude to contemplation, but it is not merely a means to something better. It is Gospel-inspired, authentic prayer.

The Jesus Prayer sets up a basic predisposition to surrender to Almighty God. Through surrender to Christ we are made children of the Father.

This is a reckless conversion of heart; a frame of mind that secures the soul in peace and freedom.

Is it really praying if we merely repeat the same words over and over? Jesus did tell us not to multiply words. But, it is not merely the words that are involved. It is the practice of the Presence of Jesus Christ in a spirit of joy that is the heart of the Jesus Prayer.

◄ ►

July 4

Unless the Lord guards the city,
the guard keeps watch in vain.
— Psalm 127:1

In 1751, twenty-five years before the signing of the Declaration of Independence, the Founding Fathers sent an order to England for the now-famous Liberty Bell. They specified that this passage from the Holy Bible be inscribed on it: *Proclaim liberty throughout all the land unto all the inhabitants thereof.* (Leviticus 25:10)

Keep in the forefront of American life the sublime concept on which our freedom depends — that we derive our rights from God, not from the State, and that the purpose of government is to protect the God-given rights of each person.

As the Declaration of Independence states explicitly: "All men are created equal and endowed by their Creator with certain unalienable rights." Today we would be more inclusive and say that all men and women are created equal and endowed by their Creator with certain unalienable rights.

Abraham Lincoln's reverent phrase, "this nation under God," serves as a reminder that we derive our rights from Almighty God.

◀ ▶

July 5

Agree with God,
and be at peace;
in this way
good will come to you.
— Job 22:21

"The centrality of Jesus in the Christian's life is a glorious truth. Each of us should ponder the depth of this union in our daily life.

"I personally believe this about Jesus Christ: that through Him I was created and called to serve.

"With Him I walk along the path of my life. In Him I find the ultimate peace on earth."
— M.G., Scarborough, Ontario, Canada

◀ ▶

> *Speak out for those who cannot speak,*
> *for the rights of all the destitute . . .*
> *judge righteously,*
> *defend . . . the poor and needy.*
> — *Proverbs 31:8,9*

Speak out — not somebody else, but you!

Speak out about injustice or instances of corruption that offend you.

Speak to your elected representatives. Write or fax them your concerns for improving your community.

Speak to your neighbors, not to complain, but to awaken them to action.

Speak to yourself and ask, "What can I do to bring peace and justice into the world?"

Speaking out against injustice is the beginning of wisdom. The next step is doing something constructive.

Not somebody else — but you!

◄ ►

> *If I do the works of My Father,*
> *even though you do not believe Me,*
> *believe the works,*
> *so that you may know and understand*
> *that the Father is in Me*
> *and I am in the Father.*
> — *John 10:38-39*

Jesus wants us to trust Him, but trust is a gift. That doesn't mean that God doesn't love the person who lacks faith and trust. God is always very close to those who are searching.

Once Jesus is accepted as Lord, life changes. The miracles of Jesus, the wisdom of His teachings, the phenomenal impact He had on His times and all generations after all serve to awaken faith, but none of these alone or combined can compel belief.

It is a grace, a gift, to be able to accept the person and message of Jesus.

If you want to trust the Lord more deeply, keep asking and this trust and faith will be given. Meanwhile, know that the very desire to believe is already a gift, one that the Lord intends to fulfill in His good time and in His own wonderful way.

◀ ▶

> *Let us therefore . . .*
> *resolve instead never to*
> *put a stumbling block or hindrance*
> *in the way of another.*
> — *Romans 14:13*

Be a light and a guide for others as Jesus was. The more we lighten the path of our neighbors, the greater becomes our own store of this precious commodity — the radiance of God's love.

If we recall that other persons are created in God's holy image, we will be more apt to give them their rightful consideration.

Not lumping people together into handy pigeonholes or stereotypes can be a tall order, but we can do it if we look beyond appearances to the real person and allow each individual the freedom to be himself or herself.

Look upon all persons with respect: men, women, children. See them all as coming from God. Honor them for what they are or can be. Help and encourage them to develop their full potential.

◀ ▶

> *Listen, I will tell you a mystery!*
> *We will not all die,*
> *but we will all be changed.*
> *— 1 Corinthians 15:51*

"Twenty years ago, I asked Jesus to come into my life, and within a short while, I gave Him my heart, and as you have probably heard (from others who have done the same) 'My life has never been the same.'

"I often ponder why I should be so filled with Jesus while others seem to have such a struggle in staying close to Him.

"I have often thought, 'How can I really witness for Jesus?' But over the years I came to realize how much of the fruit of the Holy Spirit God has increased in my life. The love I have for others today is so much more. I realize now that I witness for Him through my love. It is my greatest joy to share Him with others."

— I.M., Ocala, FL

◀ ▶

Show us Your steadfast love, O Lord,
and grant us Your salvation.
— *Psalm 85:7*

My Lord God,
I have no idea where I am going.
I do not see the road ahead of me.
I cannot know for certain where it will end.
Nor do I really know myself,
and the fact that I think that I am following
Your will does not mean I am actually doing so.
But I believe that the desire to please You
does in fact please You.
And I hope I have that desire in all I am doing.
I hope that I will never do anything apart from
that desire.
And I know that if I do this,
You will lead me by the right road though I may
know nothing about it.
Therefore I will trust You always though I may
seem lost and in the shadow of death.
I will not fear, for You are ever with me, and
You will never leave me to face my perils alone.

— Thomas Merton

◄ ►

*My steadfast love shall not depart from you,
and My covenant of peace shall not be removed,
says the Lord who has compassion on you.*
— Isaiah 54:10

Joy is not the absence of pain; joy is the awareness of the Spirit of Jesus abiding within your
soul. Some bright and happy souls enjoy the Lord
all the time.

Others seem to feel this joy only on occasion.

Some feel entirely deprived of joy. If you are
among the latter, don't be discouraged. It will
pass. Joy is not a matter of feelings anyway. It
is a matter of knowledge that you are never abandoned in your pursuit of the invisible God.

God is in love with you. Your joy in Him will
flower in time. He will ignite the fires of your heart
when it suits Him. In the meantime, don't be
afraid of your weakness. The supreme hope of
Christians is not in self, but in God. With God
all things are possible.

◀ ▶

> *Bless the God of all . . .*
> *May He give us gladness of heart,*
> *and may there be peace in our days.*
> *— Sirach 50:22,23*

A Wish For You

I do not wish you joy without a sorrow,

Nor endless day without the healing dark,

Nor brilliant sun without the restful shadow,

Nor tides that never turn against your bark.

I wish you love, and strength, and wisdom,

And gold enough to help some needy one,

I wish you songs, but also blessed silence,

And God's sweet peace when every day is done.

— Author unknown

◄ ►

July 13

Greet one another with a kiss of love.
— 1 Peter 5:14

"Not only is Jesus my Savior, He is my dearest friend. I can talk to Him in any given moment and He's there.

"Someone said to me once, 'I don't feel worthy.' And I said, 'You don't feel worthy? Are you saying all that suffering Jesus did dying on the cross was all for nothing?'

"I feel worthy only because of grace and God's goodness. Only to see His face, to kiss Him and to say, 'I love You.' "

— D.M., Red Bank, NJ

◄ ►

O Lord ...
let me live that I may praise You.
— *Psalm 119:174,175*

If you wish to be a person of strong character, develop powers of mind, heart and soul, be outwardly forceful and be inwardly strong. Learn the importance of praising God.

See the Church as His Divine instrument to guide, instruct and fortify you. In addition to frequenting Mass and the sacraments in your parish church, cultivate the habit of daily spiritual exercises and offer your praise to the Lord daily.

Be conscientious about such practices as morning and evening prayers, examination of conscience, grace at meals, the reading of Scripture. These will help keep you mindful that you are always in the presence of God and will gradually empower you to express your praise of God easily and naturally.

◄ ►

> *Seek the Lord . . .*
> *seek His presence continually . . .*
> *children of Jacob, His chosen ones.*
> — *1 Chronicles 16:11,13*

There are no steps in the prayer of contemplation except to place yourself in the presence of God with the simple desire to love and enjoy Him.

Instead of worrying about the worthiness of your prayer, instead of stewing over your failure to be perfect, turn within. Believe in His Presence. Enjoy Him.

God is more pleased when you enjoy Him than when you brood over your unworthiness. Be open to God's love. When you enjoy His loving Presence to you in love, you give Him great glory.

St. Bonaventure advises us to be people of desire — desire for God's Presence, God's Face.

Let your desire flow easily, without forcing feelings of any kind.

◄ ►

Each has a particular gift from God,
one having one kind
and another a different kind.
— *1 Corinthians 7:7*

"Can you tell me who made you?" the preacher asked the small boy. The youngster thought a moment. Then he looked up at the preacher and said, "God made part of me."

"What do you mean, 'part of you'?"

"Well," answered the boy, "God made me little. I grew the rest myself."

"Growing the rest" is a lifetime job for all of us. God gives us certain gfts. It is up to us to develop them.

God has fitted each of us to live one life, our own. We find personal wholeness and joy in discovering and using the particular gifts He has given us to help make a difference in this world.

We are collaborators in creation. What you and I are becoming is what the world is becoming, according to Teilhard de Chardin!

◄ ►

> *Other seeds fell on good soil and*
> *brought forth grain, some a hundredfold.*
> *— Matthew 13:8*

"When I was growing up, the thought of Jesus horrified me. That figure on a cross represented death, and the crucifixion was simply a nightmare. I was shy and sickly with poor self-esteem. The very few religious people I met, who radiated warmth and love, came and went in my life as fast as a mosquito during a July picnic. What I needed most was love. I was spiritually and emotionally bankrupt . . .

"I started searching for the truth. I read everything from Fyodor Dostoyevski to Dalton Trumbo. At a point of despair I gave myself over to Jesus Christ and was bathed in a light of love that I cannot begin to describe without a reminder of tears and goose bumps. Problems still arrive constantly, but, with Christ as my center, they are mere paper tigers.

"Once your life is touched with the love of God, nothing is ever quite the same. He has taken me, 'a seed among thorns', and placed me in 'good soil'.

"Thank You Jesus for loving me unconditionally for all eternity, for now I can love, too."

— P.M., Forestdale, MA

◄ ►

The Spirit is the truth.
— 1 John 5:6

Actor Mike Farrell, who starred in the long-running television series, "M*A*S*H," was a recent guest on our TV show, "Christopher Close-up." I asked him about his faith, and how the Lord has touched his life. Here's what he told me.

"The Lord has touched me in every way. I'm not a religious person in the sense that I was brought up to understand religion. But I think I am a person of great faith.

"Somebody once said, 'God is love.' And if that's true, if you reverse it, love is God. Behave as if love matters. If you live in an awareness of love and truth and value, then it seems to me that you're working — you're doing what God would have you do."

He continued, "I have a very real sense of who Jesus was and is. And I've always had the feeling that Jesus provides the example of what we can do with our lives. And I can't think of a better example to which to attach one's sights. There are ways in which we can comport ourselves by demonstrating concern for others, by loving, by telling the truth, and by demanding the truth."

◀ ▶

*God did not despise or abhor
the affliction of the afflicted;
He did not hide His face.*
— *Psalm 22:24*

Hear our prayer, O Lord, for the handicapped.

Bless them in their trials, and bless us in ours. We bear a visible cross, one that is often overlooked, slighted, ignored, avoided. Often we must bear the heavy burden of discrimination. Yet we all face the same basic problems of loneliness and longing.

Protect us from harm and hurt.

Bolster our confidence and strength.

Help us to find satisfaction in what we do.

Make us eager to ease the burdens of others.

Make all of us more aware of how much love we can give with all that You have entrusted to us.

Amen

◄ ►

*I can do all things through Him
who strengthens me.*
— *Philippians 4:13*

"Everyone kept telling me to change.

"I resented them and I agreed with them, and I wanted to change, but simply couldn't, no matter how hard I tried.

"What hurt the most was that, like the others, my best friend kept insisting that I change. So I felt powerless and trapped.

"Then one day he said to me: 'Don't change. Don't change . . . I love you as you are.'

"I relaxed. I came alive. And suddenly I changed!

"Now I know that I couldn't really change until I found someone who would love me whether I changed or not."

— from "The Song of the Bird"
By Anthony de Mello, S.J.

Help me, Lord, to recognize Your constant, unchanging love.

◀ ▶

> *God has made everything*
> *suitable for its time.*
> *— Ecclesiastes 4:11*

"Jesus preached on the mount. I feel He was also trying to tell us to take time out to enjoy the beauty of the universe, too.

"We always say 'time flies'. When Jesus preached He didn't rush through what he had to say.

"We feel time flies because we are always worrying about tomorrow. Jesus told us not to worry about tomorrow.

"He will take care of us."

— A.C., Ocean, NJ

Fight the good fight of the faith.
— 1 Timothy 6:12

There may be someone you know whose heart is disposed to receive the truth but who has never had it presented in a personal way by a friend.

It may be that God wants that person to hear it from you. Are you holding back when you might be radiating the warmth and love of Christ?

Think of this breathtaking possibility: You bring the faith to just one person; they, in turn, take it to one person, who takes it to another, and another. Your one effort can multiply over the years and through the generations to embrace thousands.

Now multiply your one effort by millions of others who could do the same thing.

Reflect on how we all can reach others with the message of Christ. Then act without fear. Bring your faith and love to the world.

◄ ►

Ah, you are beautiful, my love;
ah, you are beautiful.
— Song of Songs 1:15

You are loved. How wonderful it would be if you believed that truth without reservation.

May I ask a few personal questions to help you to look within? What is it that is crushing your joy right now? Why does that make you unhappy? Explore the answer more deeply.

Do you blame yourself in some way? Do you say things like, "There must be something wrong with me," or "I'm not a good person"? Do you really believe such things? If you really do believe it, then what are your reasons for this belief?

Why do you sabotage yourself? Why do you draw conclusions about yourself that are so damaging to your happiness? Don't you know you are loved? Believe that happiness is possible because it is!

Begin to live gladly because of the knowledge that God loves you as you are, totally, absolutely, without reservation.

In God's eyes you are beautiful. You are His beloved!

◀ ▶

Come to Me, all you that are weary
and are carrying heavy burdens,
and I will give you rest.
— Matthew 11:28

Is concern over the past or the future a major source of stress in your life? Consider the conclusion reached by a woman who realized that her fears were ruining her peace of mind.

She made a tabulation of her worries, estimating as well as she could their nature and origin. These were her conclusions:

40% will never happen; 30% are about old decisions which I cannot alter; 12% are others' criticism of me, most of it untrue; 10% are about my health, which gets worse as I worry.

Only 8% are legitimate since life has some real problems to meet. So, 92% of these worries are unproductive.

What would your worry balance sheet look like?

You don't have to struggle with fears alone. Cast all your cares on the Lord. God will free you from needless anxiety if only you decide to trust Him.

◀ ▶

Joy and gladness will be found in Zion,
thanksgiving and the voice of song.
— Isaiah 51:3

"Jesus revealed Himself to me as Lord and Savior. Since then it has been my privilege to walk with Him in a daily relationship.

"I believe that Jesus is truly the Son of God, born of the Virgin Mary, that He died for my sins, and rose from the dead.

"God is within me, from my morning offering, to my work as a nurse, a mother, a CCD teacher, and a wife. He has given me a profound sense of joy and peace."

— P.S., Highlands, NC

◀ ▶

> *The people who are loyal to God*
> *shall stand firm and take action.*
> — *Daniel 11:32*

Jesus was a doer, not a worrier. Your awareness of the basic issues confronting humankind is the first step toward helping to solve them. After knowledge comes action.

Each of the great problems facing the world today needs the solicitous concern of the followers of Christ, because every phase of public and private life affects our destiny.

The need is urgent and the stakes are high. Countless people all over the earth are looking desperately for the leadership that should be coming from the followers of Christ. Without us, many of God's children can become the easy prey of those who are looking to use and abuse them.

It is still God's world. He wants it to be run by people who will truly represent Him.

Anyone that takes to heart the problems of humankind and attempts to find even the smallest solutions is on the way to becoming a true carrier of God's love and a vital force in helping to change the world for the better.

◀ ▶

God delights in showing clemency.
— Micah 7:18

During the Olympics we are reminded of the superhuman effort athletes make to prepare for their particular event. Nothing is left to chance. Years of careful conditioning and training are behind each competitor's quest for glory. They hope to give the performance of their life in order to win an Olympic medal. All is endured because the athlete has a clear goal.

In this life our goal is heaven, endless union with God. Yet we already possess it here and now by faith! St. Catherine of Siena said, "All the way to heaven is heaven."

Here and now God gives us the certainty of His protection and the comfort of His unconditional love.

We need only accept His gifts of love and mercy.

And desire to live His will.

God Himself is the prize we seek, and He has already bestowed it.

◀ ▶

> *Their days are like a passing shadow.*
> *— Psalm 144:4*

Are you so busy that each today passes you by?
Read these lines written by the Indian poet and
dramatist Kalidasa some 1,500 years ago:

Listen to the Exhortation of the Dawn!
Look to this Day!
For it is Life, the very Life of Life.
In its brief course lie all the Verities and
Realities of your Existence:
    The Bliss of Growth,
    The Glory of Action,
    The Splendor of Beauty,
For Yesterday is but a Dream,
And Tomorrow is only a Vision:
But Today, well-lived, makes
Every Yesterday a Dream of Happiness,
And every Tomorrow a Vision of Hope.
Look well therefore to this Day!
Such is the Salutation of the Dawn!

The secret of holiness and happiness rests in
fidelity to the duties of the present moment. Enjoy your day, in the Lord.

◀ ▶

> *Jesus said . . . Do not be afraid.*
> — *Matthew 28:10*

"For thirty years, the 'standard spirituality' was sufficient. I attended Mass once a week, prayed once a day. Sometimes, I considered what Jesus would do in difficult situations, and I did it. My obedience to God came from fear of punishment.

"Two years ago, the devil began to win. My wife and I were disagreeing on more issues. Our children were uncontrollable. My job was becoming too difficult, and an addition on our home turned into a disaster. There was too much to bear, so I took a temporary job in another city to escape. My plan was to turn my back on my problems and start fresh.

"I found a Christian community. Their witness showed me that my needs had outgrown this one-size-fits-all faith. I was so busy trying to fix problems in other people, mine were going unresolved. I blamed others for my failures. I needed a savior, and it was Jesus.

"Now I see Christ in others more clearly. Now, I don't see 83-year-old Ruth sitting alone in church fumbling with the hymnal, I see Jesus. This relationship helps me to be Jesus for others, because He lives in me."

— J.S., Delmar, NY

◄ ►

*Unless you change and become like children,
you will never enter the kingdom of heaven.
Whoever becomes humble like this child is the
greatest in the kingdom of heaven.*
— *Matthew 18:3-4*

There's no doubt that Jesus required maturity
in His followers — to carry their crosses; to seek
justice; to accept persecution for the faith; to
persevere to the end.

By urging us to *become like children,* He wanted
us to become responsible, believing adults. To do
this is not necessary to lose the winning qualities
of children, the lack of self-consciousness or the
wonderful spirit of playfulness and trust.

To maintain a balance between growing up and
maintaining the outlook of a child is the work
of grace. But Jesus Christ promised all the grace
we need. We have only to ask. He assured us we
would never be alone.

◄ ►

July 31

*Mary, the sister of Lazarus and Martha,
sat at the Lord's feet and
listened to what He was saying.*
— *Luke 10:39*

Mary chose the contemplative way. It is the simple way of gazing upon the Beloved.

Contemplative prayer centers on the experience of God's love. And on the Person of Jesus Christ.

You are destined for an eternity of heavenly joy. This is why you were created. This is your destiny.

Even when caught up in sin the soul is still capable of faith and love. Sins of weakness are not roadblocks. The just person sins seven times daily. The struggle to be good is ongoing.

Yet contemplation is possible anytime for the person who seeks God with a sincere heart.

The Lord loves you even as you stumble. This is why joy and contemplation are so possible, and so fitting for everyone.

You have a vocation to joy. Accept it. Sit at the Master's feet. Listen to Him, every day.

◀ ▶

August 1

Whenever we have an opportunity,
let us work for the good of all.
— *Galatians 6:10*

There's an old proverb that runs: "The road to hell is paved with good intentions."

It is relatively easy to concoct lofty plans for anything from self-improvement to changing the world for the better.

But following through on those noble aspirations to actual performance is something else again. The temptation to postpone is difficult to resist.

Discipline yourself to write a personal mission statement. Set down your goals and objectives in writing. Avoid putting off the fulfillment of good intentions. Keep them before you, and make the most of all your God-given opportunities to become a saint.

◀ ▶

August 2

*Do not withhold good from those to whom it is
due, when it is in your power to do it.*
— *Proverbs 3:27*

A little cake of yeast on the kitchen shelf
teaches us a significant lesson.

Its magic life-giving power to turn inert dough
into wholesome, palatable bread is a graphic
reminder of the dynamic potential of the grace
of God within you.

For centuries, yeast had been a source of wonder and speculation. But it was not until 1857 that
Louis Pasteur painstakingly proved that its transforming powers stem from the fact that it is a living organism.

He conclusively demonstrated that a living
thing must always be the starting point for the
production of more living matter.

But the "live" cake of yeast must be in the midst
of inert dough to do its energizing work. It affects
nothing so long as it remains on the shelf in its
wrapper.

Just as a small cake of yeast can leaven or acti-
vate a great mass of dough, so can one person
like you stir up the grace you've received in Baptism, Confirmation, Marriage or Holy Orders. Act
as a leader, transforming a world that is waiting
for the gifts that only you can bring.

◄ ►

> *The steadfast love of the Lord*
> *never ceases.*
> *— Lamentations 3:22*

There's a story about a traveler in Ireland, who met an elderly gentleman going in the same direction as he. They walked along enjoying the scenery together. Then a storm came up.

The two men took shelter, chatted awhile and eventually fell silent. Then the old man took out a small book and began to pray.

The traveler was deeply touched by this, and said, "You must be very close to God."

The old man paused and smiled. Then he said, "Yes, He's very fond of me."

I wish we could all believe that God is "very fond" of us like this old man. Then we could relax a bit more, leave more of our woes in His hands and have plenty time left over to enjoy ourselves and be of real use to others.

◀ ▶

Keep silence and hear, O Isarel!
— Deuteronomy 27:9

Silence is the language of God. Contemplation is the garden of our communication with God.

As an intellectual action, contemplation is a silent inner gazing upon the Lord by dwelling in His silence. God's love, His Presence, His beauty, is apprehended and understood by intuition. You look at Him and He looks at you, but not with the eyes of the body. It is a spiritual gazing, a wonderful awareness of God's Presence.

Contemplation, viewed from the perspective of the heart, is the inflowing and outpouring of love. It is the highest act of love. Mind, will and heart fuse into one simple, unselfconscious act. The self is lost in the loving.

Even if it is only for a few seconds, the gift of contemplation is an experience of joy that will nourish every other action throughout the day.

◄ ►

August 5

The bee is small among flying creatures,
but what it produces is the best of sweet things.
— *Sirach 11:3*

God can use everyday acts of kindness to shape
our own and others' lives.

Drops of water
grains of sand —
    with time and unrelenting persistence
    carve monuments in stone
    no human effort can match.
So with our lives —
    the fleeting thoughts
    the momentary inspirations
    the beauty seen
    the verse read
    the smile given
    the hurt ignored
    the harshness unsaid
These small disciplines and tiny joys form a life
and mold a character that outlasts all the mon-
uments of time.

— Roy Nunley

◄ ►

His speech is most sweet,
and He is altogether desirable.
This is my beloved and my friend.
— Song of Solomon 5:16

"Being a product of Catholic schools, I had the good fortune of knowing who Jesus is all my life. As I matured, my love for Christ and my desire to know more about Him grew and grew.

"Throughout the many sad periods of my lifetime, I knew that my friend was beside me, guiding and comforting me. Likewise, on the happiest occasions of my life, I felt His presence and joy. Now, at mid-life, my relationship with Him deepens. I rely on the fact that whenever I wish, I may go to Him and He will always be at home! He is the one constant in a world full of uncertainty, doubt and difficulty.

"Knowing my own human frailty, Jesus has become my source of strength. This confident friendship has enabled me to enjoy the things He has given us in this life."

— U.D., Lincoln Park, NJ

◄ ►

August 7

The joy of the Lord is your strength.
— Nehemiah 8:10

The world "joy" is mentioned in the Bible more than 130 times. Over and over again, we are reminded that God wants us to live happy lives, not gloomy or cynical ones.

If you cultivate a spirit of joyfulness especially when the going is hard, you will have good reason to rejoice. You will be God's special agent in creating positive change in the world.

Laugh at your own shortcomings. Be cheerfully patient with the faults of others; play down the scolding attitude and be a leader who inspires people in the midst of sorrow.

*Those who wait for the Lord
shall renew their strength,
they shall mount up with wings like eagles,
they shall run and not be weary,
they shall walk and not faint.*
— *Isaiah 40:31*

Lord, You once told the prophet Isaiah that those who hoped in You would have the wings of eagles.

Things are getting me down, Lord. I need those wings. I need Your strength now.

With Your love enfolding me, I know I will be able to persevere.

Enable me to trust in You, Lord.

And, please, give me the wings of eagles so that I can soar and not be weary.

Amen.

◀ ▶

Lord, You have been
our dwelling place in all generations.
— Psalm 90:1

Prayer is not a stratagem for occasional use, a refuge to resort to now and then.

(Prayer) is rather like an established residence for the innermost self.

All things have a home; the bird has a nest, the fox has a hole, the bee has a hive.

A soul without prayer is a soul without a home . . .

To pray is to open a door where both God and the soul may enter.

— Rabbi Abraham Joshua Heschel

◀ ▶

From His fullness we have all received,
grace upon grace.
— *John 1:16*

"Several months ago, I abandoned myself of this life on earth and totally gave myself to the Lord, Jesus Christ and the Blessed Mother to be a servant of their will. Ever since that time, they brought me back to reconciliation in the church. I've been able to stay in God's graces, practicing my faith and have increased my prayer life, especially saying the rosary.

"My whole life has changed for the better. Problems are easier to deal with because of fewer complications. I am in daily communication with the Lord, Jesus Christ and the Blessed Mother, by attending Mass every day, receiving Communion and letting them plan my daily assignment.

"By opening up my heart to the Lord, Jesus Christ and the Blessed Mother, they have filled it with the Holy Spirit and are guiding me on the right path."

— A.M., Indialantic, FL

◄ ►

August 11

Be imitators of God, as beloved children,
and live in love, as Christ loved us.
— Ephesians 5:1-2

What does it mean to really practice our faith?
That's a good question. God has given each one
of us a unique combination of gifts and talents.
A treasure unlike anyone else's. And Jesus asked
us to use and perfect these gifts in the service of
others, commanding us to love one another.

You and I are invited to become His partners
in the process of making this a better world for
everyone. Especially the least among us. And the
rewards of a life well lived on earth are a sense
of self-respect and the promise of eternal life.

So live generously. And use your talents to help
others to grow and prosper. Begin by being kind
to those closest to you.

◀ ▶

> *Just as I have loved you,*
> *you also should love one another.*
> — *John 13:34*

The love Jesus preached in the Gospels extends to all phases of life.

To those who engage in commerce of any kind, Lord, grant Your grace
   to keep the public interest ever in mind
   with truthful advertising
   trustworthy products
   and honest business practices.

To consumers, Lord, grant Your grace
   to choose wisely,
   to buy carefully,
   to live modestly.

To all of us, Lord,
   grant Your grace
   to be good stewards of all that we possess.

                                    Amen

◀ ▶

I will be glad and exult in You.
— Psalm 9:2

In his book, *The Secret of the Singing Heart,* author C. W. Naylor writes, "Humor, mirth, and playfulness are all divinely created to serve God's purpose in us, to balance the pain, the heartaches, and the tears that assuredly will come."

For Maggie Sutton, the joy provided by a pet turned her life around after the death of her husband of 40 years. Depression and suicidal thoughts had invaded her life. Then she adopted a dog.

She says, "The day I brought the dog home, I laughed for the first time in weeks. How can you watch a little puppy playing and not laugh? . . . laughing is good for your health."

Laughter doesn't indicate an attempt to deny, belittle, or cover up the pain that you may feel in your heart. Rather, laughter says, "Yes, it hurts, but humor helps remind me that this pain is only temporary." Christian joy is not the absence of pain. It is rather the presence of God within.

◄ ►

*Gideon built an altar there to the Lord,
and called it, The Lord is Peace.*
— *Judges 6:24*

"I have never reached the height of five feet.
Most people, when glancing my way, are fasci-
nated by my stature and their stares make me feel
uncomfortable. I take it as part of my cross in
this life.

"However, in looking back at my whole life, I
can see clearly now how Our Blessed Lord took
special care of me. Also, Our Blessed Mother kept
her arms about me and wouldn't turn me loose
when I was in my wild ways. She always helped
me to come back where I belonged.

"And now, my Mystical Dimension. When I go
into church and sit in front of the Blessed Sacrament in the Tabernacle, I always feel a peace which
the world cannot give. I am not short anymore,
I am not tall. These things do not matter anymore.
I am at peace."

— J.M., Avon Park, FL

◀ ▶

*Jesus Christ is the same yesterday
and today and forever.*
— *Hebrews 13:8*

"Jesus became a reality for me through Mary,
His mother. She teaches me who Jesus her Son
was for her. As I clearly hear her say *Do whatever
He tells you,* the road narrows for me.

"Forgive as I have forgiven you, Jesus tells me.
Each time I choose to forgive, Jesus fills me with
new hope, new joy. It is such a freeing experience
and something realized only when I submit to His
word. Submitting my pride hurts. To be humble
is a goal and something to be worked at each day.

"Jesus is forgiveness, love, humility, hope, joy,
strength, perseverance. Jesus is my role model and
although I choose to forget this many times, Jesus
does not forget. His word never changes. *Jesus
is the same yesterday, today and tomorrow.*"

— R.K., Cocoa, FL

◀ ▶

Whatever you do, in word or deed,
do everything in the name of the Lord Jesus.
— *Colossians 3:17*

Lord, make me an instrument of Your peace.
Where there is hatred, let me sow love;
Where there is injury, pardon;
Where there is doubt, faith;
Where there is despair, hope;
Where there is darkness, light;
And where there is sadness, joy.
O Divine Master,
Grant that I may not so much seek
To be consoled as to console;
To be understood as to understand;
To be loved as to love;
For it is in giving that we receive;
It is in pardoning that we are pardoned;
And it is in dying that we are born to eternal
life.

— Attributed to St. Francis of Assisi

◀ ▶

All have sinned and fall short
of the glory of God;
they are now justified by His grace as a gift,
through the redemption that is in Christ Jesus.
— Romans 3:23-24

Failure is part of the human experience. All of us share a capacity to fail. Making mistakes or just "falling short of the mark" is part of what it means to be human.

Although we are created in the image of God, we are unlike Him in that we are not perfect. Our failure to meet God's standards is what Jesus came to reconcile and forgive.

Yet failure is often difficult to deal with. Owning up to our errors is not easy. Even more difficult is the attempt to rectify or undo them.

To cope with failure we need to:

■ summon the courage to acknowledge our mistakes;

■ find the humility to admit them to others;

■ seek the strength to make amends.

Allowing Jesus to become your strength is the key to victory. Turn all your problems over to Him today as an act of love and trust.

◄ ►

> *It is written, How beautiful are the feet of*
> *those who bring good news!*
> — *Romans 10:15*

"Our Lord knows that there is no merit in using the words 'virtue' and 'holiness' as brickbats to beat people over the head. Our Lord stands forever with the adulteress against those who would stone her to death; doing this, He does not encourage her sin, but understands and forgives her weakness.

"Our Lord is present in any of us who suppresses a harsh word or a rash deed for His sake. Our Lord loves us sinners not because of our sins, but in spite of them. He loves all human life: the homosexual no less than the fetus, the divorcee no less than the cardinal.

"When we encounter those who do not recognize His love, we should remember that He wants us to come to Him freely. He does not coerce us, nor should we try to force others to acknowledge Him as Lord and Savior.

"Our Lord is strong without being belligerent, tender without being weak. To spread the good news, we need not shout; we must simply live in Him and let His love live in us."

— T.D., East Boston, MA

◄ ►

August 19

Let all that you do be done in love.
— 1 Corinthians 16:14

Actress Ruby Dee was a guest on Christopher Closeup not too long ago. I was congratulating her on receiving an Emmy Award, and this is what she had to say:

"Well, it really was quite a surprise, and I was very pleased to get it. It was, to me, an expression of appreciation and love.

"God tells us He loves us in many ways," she continued. "He doesn't pop out of the sky and give us a kiss, but He will give us a husband or lover and a friend, and He will give us a body of people who will give us an award. He kisses us in many ways, and He puts people in your presence that pat you on the back and say, 'Amen' to whatever it is you're trying to do."

Ruby Dee has an interesting view on how we can find the Lord in everyone around us. Try to give one of His "kisses" to the people in your life.

◀ ▶

> *A joyful heart is life itself,*
> *and rejoicing lengthens one's life span.*
> — *Sirach 30:22*

Living gladly because of the knowledge of God's love means that the focus is always on God. Otherwise we can very easily become self-centered, driven from within. "I must do this, I must do that."

No one gets very far in spiritual growth thinking about themselves, and all they have to do. Joy is not attained through self-indulgence, or a life of religious posturing. Joy is certainly not found in anxious activity.

Jesus taught us to find joy by listening to His words in a spirit of humble surrender.

Joy will be a by-product of our intimacy with God. Joy flows from our relationship with God. Joy comes from the knowledge of His love. We merely respond to the promptings of His Spirit.

This openness to the Lord begins with faith in His love. The Lord loves each of us deeply, passionately, eternally.

◄ ►

Those who are kind reward themselves,
but the cruel do themselves harm.
— Proverbs 11:17

Conflict is universal, inevitable, as old as humankind. It begins when your needs, wants, values and ideas clash with those of others.

In and of itself, conflict isn't the problem. It becomes a problem when it is rooted in selfishness — "I want what I want when I want it" — rather than making the effort to find ways of working out differences together.

Inordinate concern for self leads to bickering, resentment and even the death of love. So often the by-product of conflict is division.

But conflict is not something to be avoided at all costs. Jesus, for instance, didn't shun conflict. Indeed, he was often surrounded by it, challenging even the religious establishment by healing on the Sabbath, for example.

In trying to settle differences, keep in mind that on the other side is a real person with genuine feelings, concerns, needs and views — someone made in God's image and deserving of respect.

◀ ▶

> *We have this hope, a sure and*
> *steadfast anchor of the soul.*
> *— Hebrews 6:19*

"Jesus loved me before I was born. He placed me in my mother's womb. He held me in my mother's arms. He brushed my hair when my dad was trying to get out all the tangles. He helped me with my homework and made me eat my dinner.

"He stood beside me when I made mistake after mistake. Even when I would not acknowledge my sins as sins, He never left my side, but waited patiently. He kept calling me. He was my sponsor when I was Baptized, when I received Confirmation and when I received the Eucharist. When I think I've reached my destination, He continues to call me.

"He was every friend I ever had, every friend I ever will have. He greets me when I enter the church. He enters my thoughts the second I am conscious in the morning. He is always with me. He is my anchor. He would never leave me. He is my heart."

— S.F., Kingwood, TX

◀ ▶

Bless Him each and every day;
sing His praises.
— Tobit 12:18

Jesus said, "Be not anxious about tomorrow, sufficient unto the day are the day's troubles."

Julius Caesar decreed that the calendar year match the solar year — 365 days, with an extra day every fourth year.

To correct errors in the Julian calendar, Pope Gregory XIII ordered ten days dropped and the new year to begin on January 1st instead of March 25th. He also decreed that every fourth year should be a "leap" year.

Calendars can number our days. But they cannot guarantee that we will put them to good use.

More of us should set aside a few minutes each day for prayerful reflection and to allow God to speak to us in silence.

◀ ▶

> *Let the little children come to Me,*
> *and do not stop them;*
> *for it is to such as these that*
> *the Kingdom of God belongs . . .*
> *whoever does not receive the*
> *Kingdom of God as a little child*
> *will never enter it.*
> — *Luke 18:16,17*

Try not to fall into the trap of thinking that you can achieve contemplation by sheer will power.

God's interior happiness is as close to you as your own heartbeat, it will overcome all obstacles and penetrate every layer of pain if you allow it.

Become like a child. Enter into the world of God's joy. It is possible if you ask because the Lord has promised it.

God's joy will come to you, perhaps when you least expect it. It may be mingled with the pain of life, but you will know when it comes.

God's love, whether you feel it or not, is present to you here and now by faith. God is with you, the same today, tomorrow and always.

Jesus said, *I have told you all this that your joy may be full!*

◀ ▶

> *Do you not know that your body*
> *is a temple of the Holy Spirit within you,*
> *which you have from God? ...*
> *Therefore glorify God in your body.*
> *— 1 Corinthians 6:19,20*

Pope John Paul I lived just under 66 years. But long enough to leave us some precious insights. Here is one of them.

"Once a man went to buy a new car. The salesman gave him some advice. 'Look, it's an excellent car, make sure you treat it correctly. Premium gasoline in the tank, the best oil in the engine.'

"The customer replied, 'Oh, no, I can't stand the smell of gasoline or oil. Fill the tank with champagne, which I like very much, and I'll "oil" the engine with jam.'

"The salesman shrugged, 'Do what you like, but don't come and complain to me if you end up in a ditch with your car.'

"The Lord did something similar with us: He gave us this body animated by an intelligent soul, a good will. He said, 'This is a good one, but treat it well.'"

◀ ▶

The genuineness of your faith,
more precious than gold
which though perishable is tested by fire,
may redound to praise and glory and honor
at the revelation of Jesus Christ.
— *1 Peter 1:7*

"When I was told my son was ill, he is a schizophrenic, my world went away. Then I was told my husband has Parkinson's disease. You would think I would give up. That's not all. I was told I had cancer in my breast which I had removed.

"Do you think I gave up? No. You know why. God was with me all the time. I feel what ever happens it's God's will.

"If you don't have faith you have nothing."
— J.S., Providence, RI

◀ ▶

Without eyes there is no light;
without knowledge there is no wisdom.
— *Sirach 3:25*

As Benjamin Disraeli said: "To be conscious that you are ignorant is a great step to knowledge."

How aware are you of what is going on in your community, country and world?

To be "aware" means to "possess knowledge, to show heightened perception, ready comprehension and appreciation."

Awareness can take many forms. It may signify, for instance, a realization of one's own personal strengths and weaknesses.

Or again, it may indicate being alive to the needs of others from your next-door neighbor to people in the far corners of the earth.

God blesses anyone who strives to become more aware of the needs of others.

◀ ▶

You are a people holy to the Lord your God;
the Lord your God has chosen you
out of all the peoples on earth
to be His . . . treasured possession.
— *Deuteronomy 7:6*

The world is filled with sorrows. Human misery is prevalent. For many the feeling of being alone and unloved is the crowning humiliation of a long, sad life. But there is a way to lighten the burden of human sorrow.

Appreciate the infinite love and warmheartedness of Almighty God. His Heart is an abyss of love. If only we could make this good news known more widely! The revelation of God's love is the essence of the Gospel.

A 19th century Spanish mystic, Sister Josefa Menendez, once wrote, "It was love that created the human family and all things which enhance human life . . . It was love that caused Jesus to be born . . . to spend 30 years in work . . . solitude and silence (to) . . . suffer . . . and die on the cross . . . to redeem the human race."

God's love enfolds you now and always. Never doubt God's love for you.

◄ ►

Do not fear, for I am with you . . . I am your God;
I will strengthen you, I will help you.
                    — Isaiah 41:10

Fear is sometimes a useful human emotion.

Nervous tension before giving a speech or going on a job interview can help you to prepare more thoroughly.

But fear can be destructive. It can get out of hand and poison your personal relationships.

Fear can smother your inner spirit and crush your motivation to change things for the better. Fear of major surgery, for instance, keeps some people from getting needed treatment.

Whether your fears are great or small, rational, or irrational, sudden or long-standing, you can conquer them with God's help. You can find the courage to face them with calmness, firmness and determination once you learn to depend on the Lord. Let Him become your strength and your joy.

◀ ▶

Build yourselves up on your most holy faith;
pray in the Holy Spirit;
keep yourselves in the love of God.
— Jude 1:20

"I have learned to walk in faith accompanied by Jesus and found how sweet is His will for me. Aside from being a wife and mother, all my adult life has been spent in the lay apostolate.

"His peace assures me that by responding positively to circumstances of each moment that I am doing what He expects of me.

"Not having a full-time spiritual director often concerns me, but Jesus always counters that the Holy Spirit teaches everyone. Spiritual reading is the mainstay He uses to speak in my mind. The best part of my day is when I hold Him in my hand and drink from the cup, knowing in a rush of faith and love that here is my God! I want only to offer Him thanksgiving and love."

— M.M., Metamora, IL

◄ ►

> *Trust in the Lord, and do good.*
> — *Psalm 37:3*

I came across the following passage written by W. Heartsill Wilson, entitled "A Prayer for Today."

"This is the beginning of a new day.

"God has given me this day to use as I will.

"I can waste it — or use it for good, but what I do today is important, because I am exchanging a day of my life for it!

"When tomorrow comes, this day will be gone forever, leaving in its place something that I have traded for it.

"I want it to be gain, and not loss; good, and not evil; success, and not failure; in order that I shall not regret the price that I have paid for it."

This day is all we have. Is there someone for whom an act of kindness could make a world of difference?

Use today well because it will be gone tomorrow.

◀ ▶

> *Lord, if another member of the church*
> *sins against me, how often should I forgive?*
> *As many as seven times?*
> *Jesus said to Peter, Not seven times,*
> *but, I tell you, seventy times seven.*
> — *Matthew 18:21-22*

Forgiveness isn't easy.

Here are a few suggestions to make forgiveness a little easier:

◼ Look squarely at the injury you have suffered.

◼ Ask yourself what pressures the person who hurt you was feeling.

◼ Think about how good it felt to be forgiven for the greatest wrong you ever did.

◼ Pray for the grace to forgive those who have offended you even if they haven't asked for it.

◼ Take some action as soon as possible to express your decision to forgive.

God our Father is extravagant. He forgives seventy times seven, meaning His forgiveness is without limit. He asks us to do the same for ourselves and for others.

◀ ▶

Whatever your task, put yourselves into it, as done for the Lord ... since you know that from the Lord you will receive the inheritance as your reward; you serve the Lord Christ.
— *Colossians 3:23,24*

Reflect on these words from Helen Keller:
"I long to accomplish a great and noble task, but it is my chief duty to accomplish humble tasks as though they were great and noble.

"The world is moved along, not only by the mighty shoves of its heroes, but also by the aggregate of the tiny pushes of each honest worker."

Never forget that the architect can accomplish nothing without the work of brickmakers and bricklayers. Work faithfully and well today, knowing that in serving others, you serve the Lord.

◄ ►

September 3

Here is . . . My chosen, in whom My soul delights.
— Isaiah 42:1

"Christ came to me at Baptism when I began to share God's life and love.

"Very young I began learning about Christ from a loving mother and at a parochial school from dedicated sisters. At fourteen Christ came to me in the Sacrament of Confirmation.

"In my nursing profession I carried Christ with me in the loving care of my patients and I saw Christ in them. Christ came to me again when I was married at a nuptial Mass. We were wedded in Christ.

"Christ came to me regularly in the Sacraments of Penance and Communion. After my mother died I began going to daily Mass as she had. At the Consecration Christ comes and I adore Him. At Communion, Christ gives Himself to me and I thank Him. Afterwards, I carry Christ to everyone. I see Christ in everyone. I do this by being active in the parish community.

"Now I show Christ to all who live here at the seniors' residence. The living flame of Christ's love is with me in life and will be with me in death."
— G.L., Latham, NY

◀ ▶

Whenever we have an opportunity,
let us work for the good of all.
— *Galatians 6:10*

One of my guests on a recent "Christopher Closeup" TV program was Dr. Vincent Fontana, medical director of the New York Founding Hospital. He has been a crusader against child abuse for many years. I asked him what Jesus meant to him, and here's what he told me:

"I would say that if it weren't for Jesus, if it weren't for the good Lord, I don't think I would be in the position I'm in. Every morning I leave my house, I ask Him to open up doors so that I can speak for children and families in His name.

"I feel that I'm God's instrument, doing His work. And I believe every person can make a difference. Every person can do God's work."

Think about what you can do in the Lord's name — help a child, feed the hungry, share your strength with a sick person. Use *your* skills to "open up doors" and reach out to those around you.

◄ ►

September 5

> *Do not hate hard labor or farm work,*
> *which was created by the Most High.*
> *— Sirach 7:15*

Your Son was a carpenter, Father.

But some people look down on those who work with their hands.

Inspire those in factories, on farms and in machine shops to put their hearts into what they do. To take pride in the products of their toil.

Let your work be a prayer, offered with a humble and contrite heart.

You couldn't have a better example than the Carpenter from Nazareth, God's Son.

Amen

◄ ►

> *Teach me Your way, O Lord,*
> *that I may walk in Your truth.*
> — *Psalm 86:11*

How can I listen to God?

To listen means to be alert, open, quiet. God speaks to us in many ways: in the beauty of His world, in the pain of life, in the comfort others offer, and in their call for help.

I listen for His guidance. I ask Him to tell me where I fit into His plan.

I listen for clues as to how I can make the world around me a better place.

I listen so I'll know what it means to be a carrier of divine love.

◄ ►

You clothed me with skin and flesh,
and knit me together with bones and sinews.
You have granted me life and steadfast love.
— Job 10:11-12

"Jesus is my life, my liberator, best friend and King. I realize now that He has watched over me even in the womb. As the mother of four, I know it wasn't I that knit their bones and gave them sight, speech and the gift of wisdom.

"I call on Our Lord in times of need but am learning to see His presence in all things. I pray for the intercession of the Blessed Virgin Mary. He gave her to us as His last gift on the cross and when I go to Jesus in this way my crosses are lighter.

"In my sinfulness I fail Him, but He forgives and encourages me in His way.

"I was timid, but in Him I am empowered. Because of Him I am. Without Him I am nothing. He is my hope. In Him I place my faith. And His love casts out all my fears."

— S.H., Flatrock, NC

◀ ▶

> *Do what is right and good*
> *in the sight of the Lord.*
> — *Deuteronomy 6:18*

Cicero, the Roman orator and statesman, set forth what he considered the six most drastic mistakes made by people in the course of their lives. They are:

■ The delusion that individual advancement is made by crushing others.

■ The tendency to worry about things that cannot be changed or corrected.

■ Insisting that something is impossible because we cannot do it ourselves.

■ Refusing to set aside trivial preferences.

■ Neglecting development and refinement of the mind, and not acquiring the habit of reading and study.

■ Attempting to compel others to believe and live as we do.

These mistakes did not cease to exist with the fall of Rome. We're still making them.

With God's help, we can move a little further along the road to a balanced, fair-minded view of reality.

◄ ►

> *There is a tree of life for those*
> *who do God's will.*
> *— 4 Maccabees 18:14*

There is a tale of two Buddhist monks. One prayed all day long in somber silence. A second sang God's praises joyfully as he danced around a huge sycamore tree.

One day an angel appeared to both saying, "I have come from God and you have permission to ask Him one question." Each in turn asked, "How many more lives must I live before I will attain self-realization?"

One week later the angel returned. To the first monk he said, "You must live three more lives." That monk broke down in tears.

Then the angel told the dancing monk that he had to live as many more lives as there were leaves on the sycamore trees. "Why there must be 10,000 leaves." He paused for a moment and burst into a smile, "Only 10,000 more lives and I will attain self-realization!" And he sang and danced even more exuberantly.

Suddenly the voice of God thundered, "My son, this day you have attained self-realization!"

In total acceptance is the moment of total liberation. In His Will is our peace.

◄ ►

I was in prison and you visited Me.
— *Matthew 25:36*

Jesus speaks clearly about the importance of tending to the needs of others. He tells us that when we feed the hungry, clothe the naked, and visit the sick or imprisoned, we in fact feed, clothe and visit Him.

However, the needs of others are not always easily recognized. Often we are called to meet emotional or spiritual needs which are hidden from the eye.

For instance, people can be imprisoned by anger, greed, loneliness and self-hate. They need help, too.

- Contact a shut-in by phone just to talk.
- Send birthday or holiday greeting cards.
- Assist a person with low self-esteem by suggesting a self-help group or a counselor.
- Help a prisoner of doubt by providing good spiritual reading from your personal library.

Let us pray for the insight to recognize the hidden needs of those around us.

◄ ►

September 11

*Guard the good treasure entrusted to you,
with the help of the Holy Spirit living in us.*
— *1 Timothy 1:14*

"My relationship with the Lord is my greatest
treasure. My childhood was unpleasant, very confusing and unhappy. The one person I had was
Jesus. He has always been in my life even when
I was not aware of Him.

"He was the only person that I could go to and
talk, cry or ask for help and find comfort. I felt
'listened to,' and I 'belonged' to Someone who
knew me and still loved me.

"I am at home with the Lord, a peaceful home,
a loving home, where I can be myself and where
all my faults are accepted anyway.

"He guides and leads me, doesn't use force and
doesn't criticize me. He speaks softly but yet He
lets me know when I am off base and He hauls
me back on the right road. I trust in His directions because He has never misled me, lied to me
or hurt me.

"He has never abandoned me and He gives me
the freedom to be me with all my faults."
— J.D.F., Townsend, MA

◀ ▶

Above all, pray to the Most High,
that He may direct your way in truth.
— Sirach 37:15

Jesus is the way.

People have offered many definitions of the way to happiness: wealth, power, fame, virtue — just to name a few.

Lao-Tzu, a sage of ancient China, gave his view:

"He who understands others is learned.

"He who knows himself is wise.

"He who conquers others is strong.

"He who subdues himself is stronger."

For Lao-Tzu everything depends on "self." But for those who follow Jesus, everything depends on Him.

Amidst the conflicting and confusing demands of home, office, school or community, we can too easily fall into the trap of egocentric living. But there is one simple answer: turn to Jesus.

Try to set aside at least a few minutes each day to give yourself to Jesus and share your responsibilities with Him. Then you'll be able to return to a busy world with renewed vigor, sustained by His strength.

◄ ►

His father saw his younger son and was filled
with compassion; he ran and put his arms
around him and kissed him . . . The father said
to his servants, 'Bring out a robe — the best one —
. . . put a ring on his finger and sandals
on his feet. And get the fatted calf and kill it,
and let us . . . celebrate; for this son of mine
. . . was lost and is now found!'
— Luke 15:20,22-24

The power to forgive is the first skill of genuine love.

When I ask for forgiveness, God's mercy covers me completely. To accept God's forgiveness is to choose to forgive and love myself.

Sometimes we have to learn to forgive ourselves before we can forgive others.

Forgiveness is not sentimental, not condescending, not righteous. Above all, it is not conditional. God's love is pure. Our love is not. Sometimes we act like a petulant child saying, "I'll forgive you if you'll apologize."

God the Father is different. God the Father loves and forgives without bargaining, without conditions. He accepts us as we are. This is what He asks us to do for one another.

◀ ▶

Honesty comes home to those who practice it.
                                    — *Sirach 27:9*

It isn't easy to be honest all the time. To know what my real intentions are. To admit my true motives.

But it is so easy to tell half-truths in order to avoid embarrassment or inconvenience. I excuse myself by thinking I'm honest when I'm only being tactless or self-serving.

Teach me, Lord, to face the discomfort of knowing myself. Help me to give others the benefit of the doubt.

Make me tireless in seeking to do Your will. Make me honest enough to treat the inadequacies of other people the way I would want them — and You — to deal with mine.

                                                    Amen.

◀ ▶

September 15

You have made me full of gladness
with Your presence.
— Acts 2:28

"**Jesus is Lord.** He came into my life in a very profound and wonderful way while I was in college.

"**Jesus is Love.** For me, knowledge of Jesus Christ has gone from an external knowing about Him to a *heartfelt* knowing Him.

"**Jesus is Life.** He encourages me and enriches me. Daily He renews me and helps me through the day. He shows me the way. He forgives. I actually cannot imagine living life without Him by my side. He brings me joy and peace. He is the center of my life and the life of my family. My wife and I have been raising our two children with Jesus as our foundation.

"**Jesus is Healing.** At 5 I lost my right leg below the knee to bone cancer. I know what it is like to live life physically challenged. I remember my mother once telling me that this was my cross to bear. However, with Jesus it has become a crown.

"We can enjoy life because we can enjoy the presence of our Lord."

— L.J.P., Burnt Hills, NY

◄ ►

Let us love one another,
because love is from God;
everyone who loves
is born of God and knows God.
— 1 John 4:7

It is impossible to be an effective disciple of the Lord without showing a tender regard for those most in need of God's love. Jesus asks us to reach out to those who have become mixed up spiritually, or who have met with misfortune, or become depressed, bitter or despondent.

Put love where there is no love and you will find love. The more you reach out to all people with the affection and tenderness of Christ, the more you will experience the real joy of serving as a connecting link between God and His beloved children.

Be a carrier of God's love and you will become another Christ.

◀ ▶

September 17

God will gather the lambs in His arms,
and carry them in His bosom,
and gently lead the mother sheep.
— Isaiah 40:11

There is great loneliness in the lack of intimate emotional relationships.

But there is also something called religious loneliness. It takes the form of an innate sense of separation from God.

This spiritual loneliness is a problem for young and old, married and single, male and female. This separation from the Ground of our Being is part of the human condition.

But Jesus invites us to be intimately united with Him (and through Him with the Father).

He invites us to experience His indwelling Presence and His unchanging love.

We have this opportunity and capacity to find relief from our loneliness through intimacy with a God who is courteous and gentle. Foster a heart-to-heart relationship with the Lord, and your loneliness will disappear.

◄ ►

> *Keep your tongue from evil,*
> *and your lips from speaking deceit.*
> — *Psalm 34:13*

Jesus taught us to be kind. Kindness requires that we avoid saying anything about others that is unfair, untrue, or malicious.

An unknown author had this to say on the subject of gossip:

"My name is Gossip.

"I have no respect for justice. I ruin without killing. I tear down homes. I break hearts and wreck lives.

"I am wily, cunning, malicious. I gather strength with age.

"I make my way where greed, mistrust and dishonor are unknown.

"I feed on good and bad alike. My victims are as numerous as the sands of the sea, and often as innocent. I never forgive and seldom forget.

"My name is Gossip."

We were created by God to help others; not hurt them. Jesus asks us to build up, not tear down; to draw people together in love, not to separate them by abusing the gift of speech.

◄ ►

September 19

Testify to the good news of God's grace.
— Acts 20:24

"Jesus is the God of my heart. He makes my life worthwhile. Without Him I would despair.

"I thank God for giving us His Son, Jesus, who suffered and died for us.

"Everything is grace. Everything. And it is the Spirit who gives me the grace to believe. I am so grateful!!!

"What a grace it is to know that Jesus thanks God for each of us.

"How does this knowledge affect me in my daily life? My life has taken a turn around for the better during the last two years. I believe it is grace and the Lord being with me."

— Sr. M.C.A., Pittsburgh, PA

◄ ►

September 20

> *Happy are those who*
> *(trust in) the Lord.*
> *— Psalm 40:4*

It is one thing to believe in God's existence. It is quite another to believe so strongly that you trust Him as you would your best friend.

It is one thing to believe that a circus performer can walk a tightrope.

It is another thing entirely to get on his back as he walks the high wire.

Trusting the Lord is more than mere belief. Trust is depending with total confidence.

Will you choose to let the Lord in your life today?

◀ ▶

September 21

*One who forgives an affront fosters friendship,
but one who dwells on disputes
will alienate a friend.*
— *Proverbs 17:9*

Jesus asks us to forgive *seventy times seven.*

Forgiveness is showing mercy even when the injury has been deliberate. It is easy to forgive when we can find an excuse for what was done. But forgiveness is most needed when we can't find any excuse at all.

Forgiveness is accepting the person as he or she is. It is letting go of judgments.

Forgiveness is accepting an apology. It is graciously respecting the effort at reconciliation, even when the hurt is deep. When you forgive you become vulnerable. You renew a commitment to the one who has hurt you, and that could lead to your being hurt again.

Forgiveness can be a way of life. By pardoning others for the little everyday hurts and annoyances and by pardoning yourself for your own mistakes, you grow in grace and tolerance.

But more importantly, you please the Lord who wants you to have a forgiving heart.

◀ ▶

> *I do not understand my own actions.*
> *For I do not do what I want,*
> *but I do the very thing I hate.*
> *— Romans 7:15*

Even St. Paul had guilty feelings. It reminds me of the mother who raced to the airport where her daughter was boarding a plane. The two had parted in anger and now the mother was beset with guilt and remorse.

At the airport, she asked a flight attendant to help her find her daughter so she could apologize before the plane took off.

"We've quarreled and I don't want her to leave with so much anger between us," she said.

Guilt is the unpleasant feeling we have when we're aware of having done something we believe is wrong — or failed to do what we know is right.

We shouldn't ignore guilty feelings, but neither should we wallow in guilt, endlessly blaming ourselves while doing nothing to change.

Confession is a wonderful way to free yourself from guilt. Ask for forgiveness. Make amends. Then, knowing that God has already forgiven you, try to forgive yourself.

◄ ►

I received mercy . . . that in me . . .
Jesus Christ might display His perfect patience.
— *1 Timothy 1:16*

"I am finding it very difficult to put into words a faith in God that always seems to have been there. Of course it has altered and matured over the years. As one gets older and relationships mature and a greater sense of understanding, appreciation and love develops, I rejoice in this sense.

"When I was about 15 one of the Sisters taught me a novena prayer based on *ask and you shall receive . . . knock and it shall be opened unto you.* For over 70 years this prayer has been loaded daily with my requests.

"Suddenly last year, as I came close to death, I was assailed by a fearful doubt. Was there really a life after death? Could I be saved?

"I could. The Lord I loved and worshipped and received daily was not a corpse, but a living, loving Person. If He lived after death, so would I. The whole wonder and reality of the Resurrection flooded me and I was filled with trust and confidence.

"How blessed I have been. I can now say: 'Oh rest in the Lord, wait patiently for Him.' "

— D.M.S., Pietermaritzburg, South Africa

◀ ▶

What does the Lord your God require of you?
Only to fear the Lord your God,
to walk in all His ways,
to love Him,
to serve the Lord your God
with all your heart and all your soul.
— Deuteronomy 10:12

Jesus taught us to show our love for God by loving one another.

For some people, spirituality is merely a matter of private devotions. But nothing could be further from the truth. Although it is intensely personal, true spirituality is not a private matter.

True spirituality is best exemplified by the example of Jesus. He immersed Himself in the joys and the woes of the people around Him, reaching out to the poor, the outcast and the wounded of this world. There was nothing private about the way He went about serving others.

Each of us has the power to follow His example by serving the needs of others.

Love God with your whole heart, mind and soul, and love your neighbor as you love yourself.

◄ ►

September 25

> *To act faithfully
> is a matter of your own choice.*
> — *Sirach 15:15*

A pious old man, Rabbi Susya, became fearful as death drew near. Friends chided him, "What! Are you afraid that you'll be reproached because you weren't Moses?"

"No," the rabbi replied, "that I was not Susya, the man I was born to be."

When you are about to make a decision, you can look to see which way the wind is blowing; you can adopt someone else's choice; you can check precedent; you can do what you think others expect of you, or in the final analysis you can be true to yourself.

God has given you the power of free choice. He offers guidance through the voice of your conscience. But you must decide whether to heed or ignore it.

◀ ▶

September 26

> *(Jesus) had compassion for them
> and cured their sick.*
> — *Matthew 14:14*

How can you help someone cope with illness?
Begin by trying to become a healing presence.

Henri Nouwen, author of REACHING OUT,
says, "We are all healers who can reach out and
offer health. And we are all patients in constant
need of help."

In the sickroom, a busy doctor or nurse, though
professionally competent, may not be a healing
presence. While a caring relative or friend might
without even trying provide a strong healing presence. Anyone can become a healing presence.

Treat the sick person as another Christ, not a
"patient." Listen — really listen. Share feelings
honestly instead of pretending everything is all
right. Be sensitive to the person's needs and
wishes.

◄ ►

September 27

Happy are those who trust in the Lord.
— Proverbs 16:20

"Our daughter was undergoing heart surgery and early in the day I thought, 'Lord, teach me in Your way.' While she was in surgery, I closed my eyes to relax, and out of a grayness came a vision of Jesus saying, 'Trust in the Lord for He is good, for His mercy endures forever.' Then there was a vision of Jesus with His arm around me as though I were an eleven year old child saying, 'Lo, I am with you always, even until the end.'

"Our daughter did not survive the surgery, but this vision held me together and countered every dark emotion or thought I had.

"Later, I considered birth control for this was the second child we had lost to birth anomalies. As I was approaching communion during this time of prayer and uncertainty, I was led to say an act of contrition, and when I finished I heard interiorly, with great authority, 'I am the Author of Life.' My prayer was resolved.

"These events led me to become active in the pro-life cause and our local Birthright."

— C.R., Red Bank, NJ

◄ ►

> *He put a new song in my mouth,*
> *a song of praise to our God.*
> — *Psalm 40:3*

Actress Shelly Fabares, who stars on the hit series, "Coach," appeared with her husband, actor Mike Farrell, on our TV show "Christopher Closeup." I asked her about the effect her faith has had on her life.

"I was born and raised a Catholic, as was Mike. And I find I have now, at this time in my life, I think the most personal relationship with God that I've had ever. It's a less structured relationship than it was.

"Being raised a Catholic, I went to Catholic school, went to Mass every day. For me, during those years, it seemed quite distanced at times.

"But in these years, it has become a profound and daily experience of my life. I have long conversation with God. Just real talks. I decided that the way that was comfortable for me to pray was to say, 'God, hi, it's me again. Here I am. Now, we really have to talk.'

"It makes me feel very close to Him. I feel a great spiritual connection to God. He's really right there for me, hears me, answers me, and talks to me. It's a profound experience, not something that I had earlier."

◄ ►

*Creation waits with eager longing ... in hope
that the creation itself will be set free ... and
will obtain the freedom of the glory of the
children of God ... We ourselves ... groan
inwardly while we wait for adoption, the
redemption of our bodies.*
— *Romans 8:19,20-21,23*

The service of love is so often a kind of waiting.
God waits.
The world He made waits.
Winter waits for spring.
Buds wait for warmth.
The earth waits for rain.
Waiting is one of the primary laws of nature.
Nothing in life comes to instant maturity. All
things begin as tiny seeds, waiting to grow to full
maturity.

Dante described hope as "waiting with cer-
titude."

God waits. Creation waites. We wait. There *is*
ultimate meaning to our waiting with hope.

◀ ▶

Faith by itself, if it has no works, is dead.
— *James 2:17*

Father James Keller, founder of The Christophers, wrote:

"Action should spring out of reflection and prayer. The minds sees: and with the help that God supplies, the will is moved to do.

"Your every effort at prayer deepens and strengthens your spiritual power. As your spiritual power is deepened, you will desire more and more to bring something of that power to others."

Jesus taught that human beings are one family under the Fatherhood of God. The prayer that Jesus taught begins "Our Father," not "My Father." All the petitions in this prayer are in the plural.

Like the members of any family, we need to care about each other, to take responsibility for one another.

Faith without charity is dead.

◀ ▶

October 1

May our Lord Jesus Christ . . .
comfort your hearts and establish them
in every good work and word.
— 2 Thessalonians 2:16,17

"Jesus understands my physical and emotional pain, my loneliness, my longings as well as my joys.

"When I wake during the night and every anxiety and terror surfaces as they often do in the dark hours, I kneel with Jesus and imagine how He must have felt at the agony in the garden. His fear and dread and uncertainty must have been as mine!

"Jesus accepts and loves even the parts that I try to hide from Him. When selfish and sinful thoughts overwhelm me I leave them at the foot of His cross.

"Jesus is my most intimate friend and lover, constantly at my side. No need to wait for Him to come home, answer my phone call, send me a card or return my letter. He is instant love, forgiveness and compassion! He is the fulfillment of all my heart's desires."

— M.G., Pompton Lakes, NJ

◄ ►

Above all, clothe yourselves with love,
which binds everything together
in perfect harmony.
— Colossians 3:14

Imagine the happiness on the face of Jesus when you accept His love and pass it along.

Giving and receiving is the way love works. Only those who accept love can fully enjoy its fruits.

The same is true of our relationship with God. When His love is accepted and enjoyed it always succeeds in accomplishing its purpose: to build up the Kingdom of God and communicate His happiness to all who are disposed to receive it.

Today, clothe yourself in God's love, and you will bear rich and abundant fruit.

◀ ▶

October 3

By faith Abraham obeyed when he was called
to set out for a place that he was to receive
as an inheritance; and he set out
not knowing where he was going.
— Hebrews 11:8

A life rooted in God is one filled with humility and openness to the Spirit. It's a life where God's Holy Spirit does the leading. It is a state of surrender where we find ourselves drawn to a place we never would have chosen for ourselves.

Our faith, then, is more than words. Our faith is a joyful surrender after the example of Abraham who did more than believe in God His Father. He obeyed.

Jesus obeyed in the same way. Jesus went to Jerusalem against the advice of friends because His Father asked it. He knew of the danger, but He went anyway.

Jesus asks us to act upon His words to *love one another.* We know we can do this because, with God's help, everything is possible. The challenge is getting ourselves in that frame of mind where we can truly enter into His life and trust in His strength.

◀ ▶

This day atonement shall be made for you,
to cleanse you; from all your sins,
you shall be clean before the Lord.
— *Leviticus 16:30*

The Jewish holy day of Yom Kippur is a day for correcting ones wrongdoings. The Talmud teaches that there are two kinds of wrongdoing: between humans and God, and between humans.

God, however, wants everyone to live in harmony. Therefore to be right with God we need to be right with our neighbors.

And so God will not hear the prayers of those who hurt others and continue in this wrongdoing. Therefore, He asks that the guilty go to those they have offended and right the wrong. Only then will God hear their prayers and forgive them.

Our God is a god of right relationships between Himself and us, but especially between ourselves and our neighbors.

◀ ▶

October 5

I blessed the Most High, and praised and
honored Him who lives forever.
— *Daniel 4:34*

"I am so glad I can tell you who Jesus is in
my life.

"I love Him with my whole heart and soul.

"Every time I pass the holy water fountain in
my bedroom I tell him that He is my breath, my
life and without Him I am nothing.

"He has forgiven my sins. He loves me much
more than I can presently imagine. He is truly my
Redeemer, my Savior. I ask for things I cannot
do and He answers me.

"When I think about this beautiful earth with
birds, flowers, people, with food to eat and water
to drink, I am completely amazed.

"I had a fractured hip and I know He will let
me walk again so that I can attend the Liturgy
daily and help those people who are less fortunate
than I am.

"I go to sleep praying and find myself praying
when I wake up. I love life and everybody around
me. But above all I love Him. He is my life and
my hope."

— M.S., Miami, FL

◄ ►

> *Do not neglect to do good*
> *and to share what you have,*
> *for such sacrifices are pleasing to God.*
> *— Hebrews 13:16*

Most good people around the world don't know how to express themselves, or to get into circulation the good ideas that God has given to them.

Here are a few ways to improve your power to communicate ideas:

Be sincere. Tell it as you see it.

Remember your importance as a connecting link between God and others. You may be the only transmitter of some truth to a person who would never have heard it if it weren't for you.

Don't be discouraged if you express yourself awkwardly. If your sincerity shines through, that is what will count. The more you try to be true to your heart, the better you'll become as a carrier of divine truth.

You will never stimulate others to action if your words come only from your lips and not from your heart.

◀ ▶

> *Abide in Me . . .*
> *Those who abide in Me and I in them,*
> *bear much fruit.*
> *— John 15:4,5*

Everything can give glory to God, if you have the desire to abide in His love.

Canadian Dorethea Monteith learned to spread friendship and encouragement to thousands of lonely shut-ins even though she herself has been using a wheelchair for years.

Each day she spends several hours mailing a newsletter, poetry and encouraging notes to aged and handicapped people she has never met.

She obtains their names and addresses from magazines for shut-ins and from friends who write or visit.

Often she includes some small item such as a bookmark.

Of her own troubles, she says, "I feel the Lord has permitted me to be a shut-in for His glory."

◀ ▶

October 8

The kingdom of God . . . is like a mustard seed,
which, when sown upon the ground,
is the smallest of all the seeds . . .
yet when it . . . grows up
it becomes the greatest of all shrubs.
— Mark 4:30,31,32

Little things make a difference.

Richard Levangie, writing in The Catholic Digest, tells of his despondency at age 19 after the death of his father, three other relatives and a close friend.

One day, feeling especially empty, he went to Mass in a strange church and sat off to the side, barely participating.

He remembers that at the sign of peace, "Two elderly women hobbled over to my solitary corner on fragile legs.

"Their journey seemed to take forever, and yet their greeting was warm and caring.

"In the short time it took them to reach me, I made the decision to rejoin the living."

Through your small kindnesses God can give someone His kiss, His hug, His hand, and His love.

Don't be afraid to reach out to someone in need today.

◀ ▶

Like clay is in the hand of the potter . . .
so all are in the hand of their Maker.
— Sirach 33:13

"When I was a child and a teenager I thought of my religion as not much more than a ritual. It was fun to meet people that I knew in church, but I did not meditate on the meaning of the Mass. Sometimes I even got bored at Mass.

"Later I married, but the fellow I married was not too serious about any religion. After about eight years he starting living with another woman and I separated from him. Since reconciliation appeared to be out of the question, I later decided to get a divorce and live at home.

"My parents often said the rosary together, so I joined them. They went to church every Sunday and I often went with them. My three daughters got in the habit of also going to church. I was beginning to appreciate the faith and to look into the meaning of the Mass.

"If most of the people in the world took their religion seriously and allowed the Lord to work in their lives like the potter with the clay, the world would be a much happier place."

— V.B., Washington, DC

◀ ▶

*Without faith it is impossible to please God,
for whoever would approach Him must believe
that He exists and that He rewards
those who seek Him.*
— *Hebrews 11:6*

Seeking the Lord and building up your Christian character is a work of grace, but don't ask for tomorrow's graces today. Turn your fears over to the Lord today and let Him carry your burdens for you.

Turn your face toward the sun, God's smile, and grow toward Him. Believe that you are God's delight, even though you are far from perfect.

Get used to the idea that God's favor is upon you. It will make a tremendous difference in your attitude toward pain, temptation, and the trials of life.

You won't want to displease God. You'll want to delight Him. And what makes all of this so wonderful is that, by desiring to please the Lord, you are already doing just that.

◄ ►

October 11

Happy are those . . . who have not
given up their hope.
— *Sirach 14:2*

Jesus was a Man of hope. He waited upon His Father's will in all circumstances.

HOPE looks for the good in people instead of harping on the worst. It opens doors where despair closes them. It discovers what can be done instead of grumbling about what cannot be done.

HOPE regards problems as opportunities. It neither cherishes illusions nor yields to cynicism. It sets big goals and is not frustrated by repeated difficulties or setbacks.

HOPE puts up with modest gains realizing that "the longest journey starts with one step." It accepts misunderstandings as the price for serving the greater good.

HOPE helps one to be a good loser because it has the divine assurance of final victory.

Father James Keller, M.M., founder of The Christophers, concluded, "HOPE draws its power from a deep trust in God and the basic goodness of human nature."

◄ ►

October 12

Why are you afraid, you of little faith?
— Matthew 8:26

Worry never built a bridge, won a battle or baked a cake. We should have some concern about the future but not a frantic preoccupation with it.

Concern that leads to effective action is one thing. Mere fretting that does little more than make a bad situation worse is quite another.

As someone wisely observed: "Worry is the interest we pay on trouble before it is due."

Rather than let needless anxiety give you grey hairs or ulcers, do what you can to face up to the challenges at home, work, or school.

If you do your best and leave the rest to God, there is little danger that you will be overcome by fear. Fear only frustrates your life. It adds nothing to your happiness.

◀ ▶

Then their eyes were opened,
and they recognized Him.
— Luke 24:31

"Through all of my folly, through all of the things that might be called triumphs, and through those things that made me sad — there has always been Someone.

"Once at Mass when our priest was leading us in a silent meditation I felt Someone standing right behind me, close enough to raise the hairs on the back of my neck. I couldn't resist the temptation to turn around and look . . . what did I expect to see? The sensation vanished.

"Was this a momentary sensation brought on by a moving liturgy? Maybe. But really He has always been there standing right behind me, catching me when I fell, calling me back when I wandered away from Him.

"When I've been in the midst of going my own way some little thing has made me stop, almost like a tap on the shoulder. In my weakness I know sin. In my friend Jesus I know forgiveness and love.

"What does Jesus mean in my life? He is the presence, the grace and the love that has always been there for me."

— D.D., Waldorf, MD

◄ ►

> *Prepare your minds for action;*
> *discipline yourselves; set all your hope*
> *on the grace that Jesus Christ*
> *will bring you when He is revealed.*
> — *1 Peter 1:13*

If you make a continuing effort to be an instrument of God's love and peace, your pilgrimage through life is bound to be a foretaste of heaven.

This is what the Apostles did. And yet, it must have seemed an extravagant and even hopeless task for them when the Master told them: *Go out to all the world and proclaim the Good News.* (Mark 16:15)

Christ realized that it was physically impossible for them to reach the whole world during the few years of their lives. But He knew that if they were consumed with a burning desire to reach everyone, they would rise above the restricting smallness of their circumstances and perform miracles.

The more you hold fast to that same longing the more power for good you can exert no matter how insignificant you may imagine your position to be.

◀ ▶

October 15

The Lord went in front of them in a pillar
of cloud by day . . . and a pillar of fire
by night . . . Neither . . . left its place.
— *Exodus 13:21,22*

God's love is like an ever-flaming fire. That is why Jesus has called us to believe in God's infinite love for each one of us.

Here is a little prayer I wrote to encourage myself to develop mental toughness against self-pity, self-doubt, and self-rejection. I hope it will be of help to you as well.

I am not alone
    for God is always with me.
I am not afraid
    for God is my shield and my armor.
I will bear good fruit
    for God is my strength and my joy.
I will persevere
    for God will never abandon me.
I am being saved
    for God is drawing me to Him.

◄ ►

October 16

There are a variety of gifts, but the same Spirit.
— 1 Corinthians 12:4

We are not all called to do the same kind of work, but everyone has the same vocation: to be an instrument of God's love. The job you are called to do in this world may be center-stage or behind the scenes, but everyone has a role to play.

You are needed where you are.
As in the heavens each and every star fills
     appointed space
So you fill that place where God has need.

Oh, do not doubt —
Your hand held out to help a friend, your love
     to warm an empty heart, even your smile to
     light the dark.
Walk serene in grace;
     you are in your needed place.
                              — Elizabeth Searle Lamb

◄ ►

Love one another deeply from the heart.
— 1 Peter 1:22

"I believe Jesus Christ is the image of the Father. He is my Way to understanding God's eternal love and compassion. He is my Sacrament of the present moment as I meet Him in the Eucharist, the Scriptures, in people and in Creation.

"Daily I meet Him in those whose lives I touch. I embrace God in each person no matter who or what they are. As I experience Him, I share His presence with the poor, those in prison, victims of passion, violence, drugs, alcohol or injustice.

"Jesus is my Master Teacher in the art of living and dying. I see Him and His wisdom in the world around me. I pray to be the bread He breaks to feed the hungry.

"Jesus Christ is my intimate Friend, my Spouse, my way to the Father on the journey of life. He is my problem-solver, my care-giver, and joy-giver. He is my light in darkness. He is everything to me. I am consecrated and consumed in His service and in the mission given to me by the Church."

— Sr. L.T., Chardon, OH

◀ ▶

We are all the work of Your hand.
— Isaiah 64:8

One day you will have the consolation of saying with St. Paul: *I have fought the good fight, I have finished the race, I have kept the faith.* (2 Timothy 4:7)

When you accept a position of responsibility, don't be surprised by the troubles, problems, disappointments and misunderstandings that go with it. One man called such trials "the penalties of leadership."

Far from being disheartened by the hardships of leadership or parenthood, regard them as a badge of honor. It is usually the best possible proof that you are on the right track.

Our Lord, the Leader of leaders, constantly reminds all who would be effective Christ-bearers that they must earn their battle scars. He said frankly:

If they have persecuted Me, they will persecute you. (John 15:20)

Look beyond the heartaches and heartbreaks that you are bound to encounter. They are the lot of every worthwhile leader.

◄ ►

October 19

*Pray in the Spirit at all times in
every prayer and supplication.*
— Ephesians 6:18

Prayer is basically a conversation with the Lord.
It's your personal way of relating to your
Maker.

Prayer can be done with or without words. In
a place of worship or in the silence of your heart
as you go about your daily routine.

The important thing to remember is that God
really loves you. His love is personal and unchanging. Believe in His love. Feel it in your bones and
try to return God's love for you by giving yourself
to God without forcing feelings of any kind.

◀ ▶

> *Seek the Lord while He may be found,*
> *call upon Him while He is near.*
> — *Isaiah 55:6*

"Christ is my constant and true friend who keeps me in His sustaining hands even when the daily cares and anxieties of life cause me to forget His presence.

"There have been countless times in my life when, through events and people, Christ has reminded me of His intimacy and care. The message is clear and unmistakable in its origin. The lesson is twofold: that life and everything we have is a free and undeserved gift from God and that without the Lord Jesus Christ we can do nothing.

"Every day, I try to pray, 'Lord teach me to love You more and more every day and help me to become the type of person You want me to be.' Sometimes I feel that my prayers are not heard. Then it is hard to pray, but somehow I overcome this feeling and I feel His strength and nearness.

"It is the life of Jesus Christ in me that is the cause of my peace and joy."

— J.W., Honolulu, HI

◀ ▶

*Continue securely established and steadfast
in the faith, without shifting from the hope
promised by the Gospel.*
— *Colossians 1:23*

"The awareness of God as my Father and
Creator places Him first in my life and since He
gave me His Son, I accept Jesus as my personal
Savior.

"Each morning I meditate and offer my day
to Jesus.

"I contemplate the life of Jesus, my only hope.
I love to imagine Him as He walked on the earth,
beautiful, radiant, kind and loving. I like to think
Jesus must have smiled and laughed when, as
Scripture tells us, He urged the little children to
come unto Him. Since Jesus was happy, I can be
happy too and rejoice in the Lord.

"But life is not all happiness. So I read about
the life of Jesus in the four Gospels, His passion
and death, how he healed the sick, and worked
miracles."

— J.D., Houston, TX

◀ ▶

> *Blessed are you who weep now,*
> *for you will laugh.*
> — *Luke 6:21*

The writing of Francis of Assisi reminds us: "A single sunbeam is enough to drive away many shadows."

You don't have to be a comedian or entertainer to bring a smile to the lips of others. All you have to do is be you — the you that God wants you to be.

Child or adult — each of us needs a few sunbeams. A smile of recognition, a smile of relief, a smile of gratitude. We need the gift of laughter.

To bring it to others is no small accomplishment. And at a crucial time, a smile could change a life.

◀ ▶

October 23

Teach us how to pray.
— Luke 11:1

Jesus responded to His disciples' request by teaching them the prayer we call the "Our Father" the "Lord's Prayer."

It's a perfect prayer.

Whenever you're in emotional pain, say it slowly over and over again.

Say it, pray it right now.

Our Father who art in heaven,
hallowed be Your name. Your kingdom come.
Your will be done, on earth as it is in heaven.
Give us this day our daily bread.
And forgive us our trespasses,
as we forgive those who trespass against us.
And let us not be tempted beyond our strength,
but deliver us from the evil one.
(Matthew 6:9-13)

> *For God all things are possible.*
> — *Mark 10:27*

Your habits help to define you as a person. Some aren't important, but many are because they reflect your inner values and beliefs.

How you think, feel and act have important consequences in your relationship with God and others.

Habits can be a source of embarrassment to you, annoyance to others, or even harmful. If you habitually gossip, fail to pay attention to loved ones, interrupt at business meetings, or "fly off the handle," relationships will suffer. You will suffer.

Because habits are so much a part of your character, knowing ways to eliminate bad ones and develop good ones is invaluable.

Changing isn't easy. It takes desire and effort. But it is worth the effort.

In creating a better world, all of us need what you have to offer. Offer your best self to others and to God.

◄ ►

> *Forgive each other;*
> *just as the Lord has forgiven you,*
> *so you also must forgive.*
> — *Colossians 3:13*

"My Hero! That's what Jesus is to me. He had the generosity to become an embryo in a human woman even though He was God, the second person of the Trinity.

"He had the courage to become poor even though He owned heaven and earth. He was humble enough to do physical labor even though he was king. He had the long-suffering patience to be unnoticed and overlooked even though the Angels in Heaven sang His praises.

"He was always gracious enough to forgive insults, rudeness and name-calling; to forgive His enemies; even to forgive those who hurled insults at Him while He twisted in agony on the cross. He said, *Father, forgive them; for they know not what they do.* (Luke 23:34)

"He, Jesus, is humble, kind and gracious. That's what I try to be — just like my hero and friend."
— J.D., Cherry Hill, NJ

◄ ►

I am not alone because the Father is with Me.
— *John 16:32*

The world is full of lonely people — sitting on park benches and bar stools, in movie theaters, at the next desk, and sometimes even across the kitchen table. Loneliness is the price we all pay for being unique human beings.

Getting in touch with our own isolation is the first step toward reaching beyond it. To feel the emotional pain of loneliness is to become sensitized to it in others.

Reaching out to others in their moments of loneliness is the beginning of your own healing.

Feelings of loneliness can bring us a clearer understanding of what it means to be human.

Prayer can be of great help in times of loneliness. Remember the words of Jesus, *Come to me, all you that are weary and carrying heavy burdens and I will give you rest.* (Matthew 11:28)

Jesus knows when you are lonely and He longs to comfort you.

◀ ▶

October 27

Prayer is not only something we do on our knees. It can be a part of the way we enjoy a sunset, or the way we delight in laughter of children.

Living gladly because of the knowledge of God's love is in itself a magnificent prayer.

Consider the words of the one hundredth Psalm. It's my favorite:

Cry out with joy to the Lord, all the earth.
Worship the Lord with gladness;
come into His presence with singing for joy.
(Psalm 100:1-2)

And why shouldn't you be joyful? The Lord's love is eternal and unchanging. And it is yours for the asking.

◀ ▶

The mouth of the righteous is a fountain of life.
— *Proverbs 10:11*

Jesus was the master or righteous speech. He used the gift of speech to communicate for the good of all.

To speak with love is to contribute to the emotional and spiritual well-being of others.

Here are some especially loving phrases:

■ Good work!
■ Let me help you.
■ I forgive you.
■ Congratulations!
■ I'm sorry.
■ You can do it!
■ We're proud of you!
■ Thank you.
■ I love you.

Words spoken in love often help you effect positive change in the life of another human being. Use them generously today.

◀ ▶

*Know the love of Christ
that surpasses knowledge, so that you
may be filled with all the fullness of God.*
— *Ephesians 3:19*

"Jesus is the love of my life. I have been blessed with a large family and good friends so I have many loves, but Jesus is truly the light and love of my life.

"I believe the Lord has been drawing me closer to Him from the beginning of my life.

"I have kept a spiritual journal for almost fifteen years. As I read over the pages I can see my deep hunger for God.

"I am in awe when I think of all the Lord has done for me. He has been there through the joy and pain of the years.

"Of all the gifts that Jesus has given me I believe the most precious is the gift of gratitude for each moment, for my life, and especially for His life in me.

"I am learning how to see each person as a child of God and as my brother and sister. I fail at this so often, but I know I am changing and becoming more loving and Christ-like."

— M.G., Riverside, NJ

◄ ►

*Guard the good treasure entrusted to you,
with the help of the Holy Spirit living in you.*
— 2 Timothy 1:14

From God's point of view, you can never exaggerate the importance of you.

The sanctification of the world starts with you. How well you succeed depends on how well you understand your own importance as a child of God and as God's connecting link to humankind.

You are important because you have been created in God's holy image; you have been redeemed by the precious blood of the Savior; you are destined for heaven. You are worth more than any treasure on earth.

In addition to your divine worth, God has assigned you a special mission in life, one He has given to no one else.

No matter how small it may seem to you, it is important to Him. Be all that you can be within the context of your present set of circumstances. You are a carrier of God's love.

◀ ▶

Love one another deeply from the heart.
— 1 Peter 1:22

Whether you are beautiful or plain, rich or poor, saintly or sinful, you are loved. Consider this prayer:

Father, as the giver of all good gifts, help me to grow in love as Your Son did.

He loved all those He met — He reached out to help them, especially the ones who were most in need.

Lord, increase my ability to love as Jesus did. Help me to love my neighbor "deeply from the heart" so that I can come closer to the Kingdom of God which He preached.

◀ ▶

*Clothe yourselves with love, which binds
everything together in perfect harmony.
And let the peace of Christ rule in your
hearts . . . And be thankful.*
— *Colossians 3:14-15*

St. Augustine of Hippo, who lived in the fifth
century, described St. Monica, his mother, as
"such a peacemaker that hearing on both sides
most bitter things . . . she would never disclose
anything of one to the other, except what might
help to reconcile them."

Peacemakers —

■ heal
■ reconcile
■ cooperate, and
■ clarify

Peacemakers do not —

■ hurt
■ blame
■ control, or
■ confuse

In the Sermon on the Mount, Jesus called
peacemakers the daughters and sons of God.
That's what a saint is, one who manifests God's
Spirit for all to see.

◀ ▶

> *The Lord God will wipe away*
> *the tears from all faces.*
> *— Isaiah 25:8*

Abraham Lincoln once said: "In this sad world of ours, sorrow comes to all, and it often comes with bitter agony. Perfect relief is not possible except with time. You cannot now believe that you will ever feel better. But this is not true. You are sure to be happy again. Knowing this, truly believing it, will make you less miserable now."

We mourn the loss of those who are dear to us, but the pain passes while the beautiful memories remain.

How can we deal with the pain? It helps to recognize that the pain will diminish; that there are memories to cherish.

The great French artist Renoir suffered so much from arthritis that it was difficult for him to paint.

Once a friend said to him, "You have done enough, Renoir. Why do you continue to torture yourself?"

Renoir replied, "The pain passes, but the beauty remains."

So it is with grief.

◄ ►

> *It is out of the abundance of the heart*
> *that the mouth speaks.*
> *— Luke 6:45*

The Spirit leads us in different ways to minister to one another. Ministering is a form of evangelization. That word is a turn-off for many. In the strict sense it means, "to preach the Gospel, or to convert people to Christ." Some sects force their way on others and find that their zealous efforts are often counter-productive.

Evangelization need not be threatening. We preach the Gospel most effectively by the way we live. There are times, however, when we can and should speak up for Christ.

Standing up for our beliefs is needed more than ever in this day and age when religion is so often treated with scorn. It's a cop-out to remain passive.

It does matter if someone insults Almighty God, or Jesus, or the Church. That insult should not go unchallenged. God's friendship is personal, and friends stand up for one another.

It is a spiritual work of mercy to speak up for your faith.

◄ ►

Choose ... individuals who are wise, discerning, and reputable to be your leaders ... Give the members of your community a fair hearing and judge rightly between one person and another, whether citizen or resident aliens.
— *Deuteronomy 1:13,16*

Lord, pour Your Spirit out upon us that we may become active in the affairs of government.

May our government use its mighty power for the healing of differences among people, governing with justice, mercy and love.

Grant to officials in our local, state and national governments a ministry of service to all, not merely to a privileged few.

To our Congress, grant the grace of upholding the common good over and above the welter of competing private claims.

To our judiciary, bestow the wisdom of interpreting the law grounded in principle, not expediency.

And bless us all with the knowledge of Your love.

◀ ▶

November 5

I came that they may have life,
and have it abundantly.
— John 10:10

The best way to keep a piano in good condition is simply to play it.

Neglect impairs the instrument in many ways. Tonal quality suffers. The keys turn yellow. The felted hammers become a target for hungry moths.

The story is much the same with human beings.

Failure to develop and put to good use the abilities that God entrusts to you will cause them to deteriorate.

God wants you to live fully, to keep spiritually and mentally creative, not merely to exist. Use your gifts to help your neighbor.

Every day try to put one of your God-given abilities to work. If you do, you will help make this a better world and you will be a better human being.

◄ ►

> *But for me it is good to be near God;*
> *I have made the Lord God my refuge.*
> — *Psalm 73:28*

"Jesus calls me by name whenever I take the time to be with Him. He speaks my name as I have never heard it spoken before — with so much love. I know how much He loves me. I ask him to 'beckon to me and to take me for His own.'

"As I knelt in prayer and meditated one evening a picture came into my mind of Jesus walking through a very colorful field.

"As He walked before me, I found it necessary to run very quickly to catch up with Him.

"He stopped and turned to look because He felt my presence. When our eyes met, I felt His gentle love. There was no conversation. He picked me up, put my head on His shoulder, and held me as a father would hold a loving child.

"At that moment, I felt as though the gift of love was being poured into my cup and overflowing."

— M.L., Lowell, MA

◀ ▶

November 7

I rise before dawn and cry for help ... my eyes are awake before each watch of the night, that I may meditate on Your promise.
— Psalm 119:147,148

A construction worker describes the beginning of each day:

"I rise at 5:45 a.m. I make the Sign of the Cross, thank and praise the Lord for a new day and then bless my wife and each child, starting with the eldest, a fifteen-year-old, down to the youngest, a two-year-old. We have been blessed with nine beautiful children, and they aren't accidents. My wife and I love each one dearly. I am most grateful to God for all His blessings.

"I spend a half hour reading the Bible. I think about God's words.

"I then go off to Mass.

"Following Communion, and after a few moments of thanksgiving I go off to work thinking about the Lord's presence within me."

Indeed, here is a man who rises before dawn and meditates on God's word, an example for the rest of us to ponder.

◀ ▶

*Do not fear ... when you pass
through the waters, I will be with you ...
when you walk through fire,
you shall not be burned.*
— Isaiah 43:1,2

Three ideals inspire Christophers to act:
Everyone Has a God-Given Mission.
You have a job to do in this world that only
you can do. A healthy sense of self is directly
related to knowing your mission in life.
One Person Can Make a Difference.
Your efforts might seem insignificant to you but
they may be all that is needed to overcome some
great evil. Take courage and follow your heart.
Positive, Constructive Action Works Miracles.
Complaining can be a waste of precious time
and energy. Be positive. "It *is* better to light one
candle than to curse the darkness."

◀ ▶

November 9

You know when I sit down and when I rise up;
you discern my thoughts from far away.
(You) are acquainted with all my ways.
Even before a word is on my tongue . . .
You know it.
— Psalm 139:2,3-4

A friend is one who accepts us as we are, when we're at our best or at our worst. God is such a friend. He sees through the unreal image we sometimes present to others and ourselves.

God accepts us "as is." He understands our weaknesses, our hidden thoughts, our wants, needs, desires, everything.

So, just be yourself and talk to Him. Convert your "unceasing thinking into unceasing prayer," says writer Henri Nouwen. And, he continues, "move from a self-centered monologue into a God-centered dialogue."

This is prayer. Giving all our thoughts to God, even our anxious thoughts, opening our secret places, the corners we guard — this truly is prayer, when we talk freely, honestly to our best Friend and heavenly Father.

◄ ►

> *Come to Me, all you that are weary*
> *and are carrying heavy burdens,*
> *and I will give you rest.*
> — *Matthew 11:28*

"The Lord Jesus is my Rock and my Strength. Though often times I feel as though I am walking on thin ice, He is the Foundation upon which I stand.

"He is with me in the morning as I awake to a new day, and He is my Friend and Confidant throughout the day. He is there for me should I need to call upon Him. He rejoices with me as I offer thanks for His Divine Providence.

"He is my very present help in time of trouble. The Preserver of my life. Every breath I take, and every beat of my heart I owe to Him.

"His mercies are new every morning, and I know that I can pick myself up and start again anew because He has purged me of my sinfulness.

"There is no better Teacher for He is the Supreme Source of all wisdom. He gives me discernment as I seek to know and follow His statutes, and as I allow Him to mold me into His image."

— F.M., Pensacola, FL

◀ ▶

November 11

Blessed is the nation whose God is the Lord.
— Psalm 33:12

George Washington composed the following prayer:

"Almighty God, who has given us this good land for our heritage, we humbly beseech Thee that we may always prove ourselves a people mindful of Thy favor and glad to do Thy will.

"Bless our land with honorable industry, sound learning, and pure manners.

"Save us from violence, discord and confusion, from pride and arrogance, and from every evil way.

"Defend our liberties and fashion into one united people the multitudes brought out of many kindred and tongues.

"Endue with the spirit of wisdom those to whom in Thy name we entrust the authority of government, that there may be peace and justice at home, and that through obedience to Thy law, we may show forth Thy praise among the nations of the earth.

"In the name of prosperity, fill our hearts with thankfulness, and in the day of trouble suffer not our trust in Thee to fail."

◀ ▶

He sought the good of his nation.
— *1 Maccabees 14:4*

What this country needs is . . .

More people to inspire others with confidence . . .

Fewer to discourage any initiative in the right direction . . .

More to get into the thick of things . . .

Fewer to sit on the sidelines merely finding fault . . .

More to point out what's right with the world . . .

Fewer to keep mentioning what's wrong with it . . .

More who are interested in lighting candles . . .

Fewer who blow them out.

— Father James Keller
Founder, The Christophers

◄ ►

November 13

Pleasant words are like a honeycomb,
sweetness to the soul and health to the body.
— Proverbs 16:24

Saying "thank you" can be meaningful for both the giver and the receiver.

All of us have been touched by others who deserve our appreciation. They may be within arm's reach, or we may have to search them out. In some cases it may no longer be possible to thank them directly.

Whatever the circumstances, finding a way to say "thank you" enhances life. Our gratitude can make others happy and promote such qualities as unselfishness, patience and goodwill.

By showing appreciation to strangers, friends and family we move closer to becoming instruments of God's love.

The word "Eucharist" is derived from the Greek word for thanksgiving, and the Holy Sacrifice of the Mass is the supreme act of our thanksgiving to God for all His blessings.

◄ ►

My sheep hear my voice. I know
them, and they follow Me.
— John 10:27

"I want to tell you what happened in 1966. I was very ill, near the point of death in a dark hospital room with an aide sitting near where I lay. I heard someone say, 'She is dying.'

"I wasn't afraid, in fact I felt it would be a welcome relief from the suffering.

"Then I saw a light, a bright light about the size of candle light. Then an enormous light which lit up only Jesus. He was smiling, holding out His nail-seared hands and I knew He was Jesus. I felt that he wanted me to live. I wasn't ill much longer and was able to recover with the help of our Lord.

"Throughout the ups and downs, trials and tribulations of life since, I see God's hand in my life and I thank Him for His son, Jesus. I am on a journey and have been most fully alive since 1978 when I became Catholic. I am so happy and glad that the Church took me in as one of its sheep."

— M.W., Lafayette, IN

◀ ▶

> *Do not lag in zeal,*
> *be ardent in spirit,*
> *serve the Lord.*
> *— Romans 12:11*

Blessed is the leader who inspires faith, courage and enthusiasm.

Blessed is the leader who leads for the common good, not for the personal gratification.

Blessed is the leader who develops leaders while leading.

Blessed is the leader who considers leadership an opportunity for service.

Blessed is the leader who prays for God's guidance and strength in all circumstances.

◄ ►

> *Pray without ceasing.*
> — *1 Thessalonians 5:17*

"Paul's meaning was: Pray whenever you can. In short, hurried bursts if necessary. But if you are to be followers and co-workers with Christ, you must be women and men of prayer.

"His instructions to us are no different: the need to get beyond our own littleness, apathy or trivial concerns is still present.

"Find your own occasions for prayer . . . waiting for a stop light . . . putting a letter in the mail box . . . in a moment of exultation or defeat . . . in the eyes of a child . . . in a lover's embrace or after a stinging conflict . . . on a crowded street or utterly alone . . . where you exercise your trade or profession or in the home.

"Prayer should always be intensely individual, but it can discover an exciting new dimension when it is also communal. As much as you can, join with others.

"Prayer that is personal, loving, humble, filled with trust, eager for forgiveness, open to the movements of the Holy Spirit, and above all persevering — can do wonders, the very signs and wonders spoken of in the Bible."

— Father James Keller, M.M.

◀ ▶

November 17

Whoever pursues righteousness and kindness
will find life and honor.
— Proverbs 21:21

Your role in life at any given moment is not what determines your worth as a human being. Roles change continually.

The parental role slips away as children reach maturity. Executives retire, surrendering their position to younger men and women. People are forced by circumstances to change their careers.

What really counts is the person you are, not your role at the moment. God has given you a unique personality and unique abilities. Success in life means using these special gifts for the good of others and for the glory of God whatever your role in life might be.

◄ ►

November 18

You of little faith, why did you doubt?
— Matthew 14:31

"At a particularly difficult time in my life I began to pray once a day with much distraction at first.

"I call Jesus my 'Sweetheart.' After Communion we sit in my flower garden and I tell Him I'm the tiniest wildflower, there for His pleasure.

"Jesus is my teacher. When I sit down to plan my Sunday school lesson, I pray silently for guidance and ideas suddenly start flowing. I may have an interior spiritual question, then I pick up the Bible and it's answered!

"These are just a few 'little miracles' I've been privileged to receive through God's love and grace.

"In times of trouble, recalling these miracles helps me to place my uncertain future in His hands. I love Him so!"

— M.C., Valatie, NY

◀ ▶

I give you a new commandment,
that you love one another.
Just as I have loved you,
you also should love one another.
— John 13:34

To say that anyone is a "dedicated person" is a high tribute.

The word "dedicated" comes from the Latin term, "dedicatus sum" meaning "I have given myself."

No one can force you to give yourself to the huge task of guiding a bewildered world towards sanity and away from bedlam.

But if you do dedicate yourself to the task of carrying the love of God to the world, your whole life will take on a fuller meaning.

Jesus asks for your hands and your heart. Give yourself to Him and allow Him to express His love through you.

> *I believe; Lord, help my unbelief!*
> — *Mark 9:24*

Dear Lord,
There are times when my faith flags and I need Your help.

I know You are there on good days and bad. But my feelings are another thing entirely.

When I am exhausted, drained from meeting the demands of a busy day, I feel alone and vulnerable.

Knowing that You are unchanging love enables me to carry on, but not without a struggle. Help me in those dark moments, Lord, to radiate Your presence, Your joy and Your love. When I feel depleted and sad, help me to seek Your comforting presence.

Amen.

> *Like good stewards of the*
> *manifold grace of God, serve one another*
> *with whatever gift each of you has received.*
> — *1 Peter 4:10*

Sam Levenson, teacher, writer and humorist, offered this thought, "There's an old Talmudic teaching which says that every child is born with a message to deliver to the human race that completes the explanation of why we're here."

In other words, every person born into this world has a God-given mission, a role to play in God's eternal plan that began before the dawn of time.

While we are moving toward eternity, we are nevertheless living in the now of life. God does not ask us to withdraw from this world and wait for better things to come. He calls us to be instruments of His love, peace and justice right now.

God gave you gifts and talents to use intelligently, constructively, lovingly, justly.

You have a song to sing that nobody else can sing. Let your song be joyful and full of loving service for your neighbor.

◄ ►

Arise, shine; for your light has come,
and the glory of the Lord
has risen upon you.
— Isaiah 60:1

"Five years ago I remember kneeling in church. My marriage and family had fallen apart.

"I prayed for forgiveness and help to reconcile my family. I prayed for God's help to make the best decision for everybody involved, especially my little ones.

"Jesus, my most loyal friend, came to my assistance. I have not found another who would make me feel as secure and trustful as He. Jesus has always sent His Holy Spirit to reassure me; to urge me to go on, to try again, to be faithful."

— J.H., Orlando, FL

◄ ►

November 23

Sing to the Lord with thanksgiving;
make melody to our God on the lyre.
— Psalm 147:7

Jesus always went off alone to pray, to give thanks to His Father in heaven. In that way He prepared Himself to carry out His mission in life.

Be on the lookout at all times for every opportunity to apply divine principles to human affairs.

Start in your own community and reach out to the world as far as you can — think globally, act locally.

Act as if everything depended on you and pray as if everything depended on God.

And always, always join with Jesus in giving thanks to His beloved Father.

◄ ►

*Those who are generous are blessed,
for they share their bread with the poor.*
— *Proverbs 22:9*

Thank You, God, for hot water; for windows that let in the air; for gas and electric at the flick of a wrist; and for the comfort that greets me as I open the door on a sunny day.

Bless those who find no warmth in their family life.

Let Your blessing fall on the poor, the lonely, the frightened and the bewildered.

Let me know that in sharing what I have with those in need I am only doing what You ask of me.

Help me to see You in the least of my neighbors.

Author Unknown

Do not worry about tomorrow, for tomorrow
will bring worries of its own.
Today's trouble is enough for today.
— *Matthew 6:34*

Jesus asks you to focus your energies on today. Are you spending too much time thinking back to the "good old days" (or the not-so-good-old-days)? Or are you looking ahead too anxiously toward an uncertain future?

To live this way is to risk missing out on today. Today is the best time you have to let your light shine. Today is the best time you have to help shape a better future.

Looking back has its value if you can learn from the past, but the past itself is gone. It can never be rewritten.

Concern for the future has a place, too. Goals should be set, plans made. But the future will probably be different from anything you might have expected.

So don't let past memories or worries about the future crowd out the joy of the present moment.

Don't miss out on today!

◄ ►

I bore you on eagles' wings and
brought you to Myself.
— Exodus 19:4

"From the age of 14 to 30 I was lost in the world of alcoholism as I searched after heroes. Instead I found abuse, two treatment centers and a few psychiatric wards.

"Out of depression when I turned 30, I went to confession for the first time since I was a teenager. I walked out of the confessional feeling like an innocent young girl again. This was the turning point. I am 32 now and have remained sober. I know peace, and love life.

"Jesus is the one who saved me. That is why He is my hero.

"While making a Miraculous Medal Novena I told Mary to tell her Son He was my hero. I told her that the song, 'The Wind Beneath My Wings' was my song to Him because with Jesus I can fly higher than an eagle and I thank God every day for knowing He is there for me."

— E.C., Summerfield, FL

◀ ▶

> *Beloved, if God so loved us,*
> *we also ought to love one another.*
> *— 1 John 4:11*

Jesus taught us to put love first.

Our human tendency is to restrict our love to a few, those around us or those who think our way. But the Lord put no limits on love. In practice it should include all and exclude none.

He could not have been more explicit when He said, *I say to you, love your enemies and pray for those who persecute you, so that you may be children of your Father in heaven.*
(Matthew 5:44-45)

By reaching out in such a supernatural way we are imitating God Himself, who *makes His sun rise on the evil and on the good, and sends rain on the righteous and on the unrighteous.*
(Matthew 5:45)

◄ ►

*Delight in the Lord, and He will give
you the desires of your heart.*
— *Psalm 37:4*

Contemplation is something you've probably done many times without even realizing it.

For me, contemplation has two dimensions: receiving and giving.

■ First, I absorb God's love.

■ Then, after a while, I love God back by giving myself to Him, warts and all. Wordlessly. In stillness. With genuine delight in the company of the Lord, I rest in His love.

Seemingly there are no results. Nothing happens. Often the silence, the stillness and the lack of movement can be tedious, even boring.

But after awhile the act of taking delight in the Lord becomes an end in itself. Try it. You'll like it.

◄ ►

> *Let no evil talk come out of your mouth,*
> *but only what is useful for building up ...*
> *so that your words may give grace*
> *to those who hear.*
> — *Ephesians 4:29*

Words can hurt.

Words spoken with anger, guilt or resentment can cut deeply with lasting effect.

Criticisms, put-downs, insults — even when supposedly delivered "in fun" — hurt feelings, bruise egos, and stunt the growth of a healthy self-image.

Parents especially should consider the words they use with their children.

Let your words to others — especially to your children — reflect the love our Heavenly Father has for all His children.

Be gentle of speech, considerate and respectful.

◀ ▶

He reached down from on high, He took me;
He drew me out of mighty waters.
— Psalm 18:16

"One New Year's eve, at a Retreat House chapel, I felt desperation for the coming year. I had no supportive friends and a limited income and was forced to move to a neighborhood where a police car and anger were the norm.

"Suddenly, I spiritually experienced a vision of myself on a dangerous mountain and Christ extending His hand to me. As I climbed, Christ kept gazing into my eyes and grasping my hands. He repeated words: 'I love you. Gaze into my eyes. Never look back.' I did and my fears melted.

"Once in the dust of a warehouse sale, I discovered and bought an antique print of Christ embracing a man sinking into the sea. The comfort and love in Christ's embrace was the exact image of my vision.

"Sometimes I imagine myself gazing into His eyes. I pray with all my soul to become His lover, especially at the Eucharist.

"Dear Lord, I ask for peace and joy for myself and others."

— R.C., Schenectady, NY

◀ ▶

December 1

*Encourage one another
and build up each other.*
— 1 Thessalonians 5:11

Helen Keller, who was blind and deaf from birth, lived in a world of darkness and silence.

Instead of living as a bitter person, the Lord gave her a grateful heart, and she lived her life joyfully, with wisdom and grace.

No doubt there are times in your life when you are miserable. Life gets complicated very easily. In the confusion, feelings of joy tend to dissolve. That's why it would be risky to depend on them.

Best always to try to remember Helen Keller: for her, joy prevailed over sorrow. For her, little love offerings were more precious in times of stress.

The Lord reads hearts. He knows your good intentions. Put aside your negative feelings and learn to laugh at them. Let the Lord be your strength and your joy. Be at peace.

◀ ▶

> *In ... rest you shall be saved;*
> *in quietness and in trust*
> *shall be your strength.*
> *— Isaiah 30:15*

Some people find it difficult to pray. They ask, "How do I begin?" According to Abbot John Chapman, the answer is simple — pray as you can, don't try to pray in a way that is false for you.

Take yourself as you find yourself and begin there. Keep it simple, a conversation between you and your Lord.

Sometimes the most difficult thing about prayer is stopping everything else. It takes willpower to create a silent space for yourself.

I like to think of prayer as a place where I can reflect on the fact that God really loves me, and that I can rest in Him and trust Him.

God's language is silence.

In silence, heart speaks to heart.

◀ ▶

Peace I leave with you;
my peace I give to you.
— John 14:27

The peace that Jesus gives is precious. He gives
it totally, completely, fully. He gives Himself.

As we approach Christmas, we ponder the gift
of God's peace which is His Son, the Prince of
Peace. And why does He come?

An early Church Father, Irenaeus, explained it
this way, "The Word of God, Jesus Christ, on account of His great love for us, became what we
are in order to make us what He is Himself."

Jesus came to make you an instrument of His
peace. Today, let your soul reflect His peace for
all to see.

◀ ▶

December 4

Ask, and it will be given you.
— Luke 11:9

Jesus has assured us that our prayers will be answered.

Prayer is essentially a conversation with God. You might say it is your personal way of giving yourself to God and asking for His help.

This can be done with or without words. In a place of worship, or in the silence of your heart as you go about your daily chores.

One woman turns the writing of Christmas cards into a prayer. As she addresses each one she thinks of a particular need or problem that person might have. As she seals the envelope she offers a prayer that God will help and guide that person.

December 5

*Our mouth was filled with laughter,
and our tongue with shouts of joy.*
— *Psalm 126:2*

Laughter is not just a pleasure, says Charles Schultz, creator of the "Peanuts" cartoon. It's a necessity.

"It has long been my belief," writes the cartoonist, "that one of the things which has enabled man to survive is the ability to laugh."

Don't be afraid to give in to a smile — even in times of sadness. Life's ups and downs can't be changed — but you can change the way you deal with them.

Belief that a loving Father guides your life is in itself a good reason to smile.

Smile to yourself more and soon you'll be filled with feelings of joy.

◀ ▶

> *Teach me Your way, O Lord,*
> *that I may walk in Your truth;*
> *give me an undivided heart*
> *to revere Your Name.*
> *— Psalm 86:11*

Distractions at prayer are quite normal for saints and sinners alike.

No one can get rid of the worries of this world. If it happens to you, remember that even Jesus experienced difficulties in His prayer life at times. Remember His agony in the garden.

If your mind wanders in a million directions out of fear or distress, don't give up on prayer. You are normal. Your prayer might not be the best you think you are capable of, but it's probably the only kind of prayer you can offer at that moment.

Simply let your prayer consist of offering yourself to God, distractions and all.

And know that, like the good Parent He is, God is pleased with your efforts, no matter how they may seem to you.

◄ ►

December 7

*Learn from Me, for I am gentle
and humble in heart.*
— *Matthew 11:29*

Jesus failed in the eyes of the world, but His failure was the triumph of God's redemptive plan.

You are more than the sum of all your successes and failures!

You are certainly worth more than all the things you own. Fortunes are won and lost every day. Your dignity does not depend on success according to the world's standards. Sometimes failure serves a noble purpose. A Carmelite nun shares her view of this spiritual insight:

"A person who assumes that life must consist of stepping from success to success is like a fool who stands next to a building site and shakes his head because he cannot understand why people dig down deep when they set out to build a cathedral. God builds a temple out of each soul, and in my case He is just starting to excavate the foundation."

In the Gospel of Jesus Christ, wealth and worldly power are presented as potential obstacles to God's grace, while the childlike spirit is praised. Learn from Jesus who did not scorn the cross.

◀ ▶

*When Jesus saw His mother and the disciple
whom He loved standing beside her, He said to
His mother, Woman, here is your son. Then
He said to the disciple, Here is your mother.*
— John 19:26-27

"My life has been full of ups and downs just
like everyone else but I can still feel joyful because
I know Jesus is my brother. He will always comfort me and be there for me whenever I turn to
Him. I am never alone.

"It's a great feeling to know that I am part of
His family. I call His father Abba (Dad) because
He is my father also. I call His mother Mary and
she is my mom, too. So I don't have to worry,
my family and I can tackle anything.

"There are times when I think of the crucifixion of my brother and friend. What would I have
done to help Him if I had been there?

"I would stand before the cross and hold His
head so that He could drink some water, or I
would tenderly wipe His cut face.

"Well, I wasn't there and I couldn't do these
things for Him then. But I see Jesus in all the people I meet and I can pass His love on to them."
— C.M.S., Wayne, NJ

◄ ►

December 9

The glory of youths is their strength.
— Proverbs 20:29

It is important to let young people know that God gave them many blessings not for themselves alone but to share with others.

Remind them that they can dedicate themselves to the difficult task of raising the standards of this world by letting their light shine in such spheres of influence as government, education, literature, entertainment, and the corporate world.

Help them realize that these vital fields, which touch and shape the lives of most human beings, are of immense importance. Help them to see why the apostolic efforts of the followers of Christ can shape this world into a haven of peace and love. Above all remind them that charity begins at home.

A good home can be a powerful factor in the shaping of the future. As God's training school, it can form an endless stream of young people to go forth as modern apostles of Christ to renew and freshen the face of the earth.

◄ ►

> *Devote yourselves to prayer*
> *... with thanksgiving.*
> — *Colossians 4:2*

One way to take prayer seriously is to commit yourself to a certain amount of prayer time each day. You might consider praying before you get out of bed in the morning. You're more relaxed and comfortable then, and the pace of life has not yet intruded on your peace of mind.

During this quiet time you can give yourself to the Lord and ask His blessing on the upcoming day. Prayer after all is in the will. It is the will to give yourself, your life, to God. He in turn gives you Himself.

Remember, God loves you today, tomorrow and always. He is open to your gift of love at all times and in all places.

December 11

The Lord is my shepherd,
I shall not want.
— Psalm 23:1

"What is our Lord Jesus to me?

"I have been thinking about the many aspects of His love when all of a sudden I came across the Psalm: *The Lord is my shepherd, there is nothing I shall want.*

"I told myself: here it is, Jesus, Our Lord, is the Good Shepherd, to me and to all who try to follow Him."

— S.M., Miami, FL

*Anyone united to the Lord
becomes one spirit with Him.*
— *1 Corinthians 6:17*

"I want everyone to know that Our Lord Jesus is most gentle, most tender, most kind, most loving, most indulgent. He in turn yearns and thirsts for our love.

"When we love Him, Jesus gives us all the treasures of tenderness which are in His Divine Heart. He delights in letting Himself be possessed by a loving soul.

"Our Lord is a God of Infinite Goodness and Mercy. He will never refuse to forgive anyone no matter how numerous the sins. We have only to think of the good thief who was crucified with Jesus, and the beautiful story of the Prodigal son. No questions asked. Just complete forgiveness. All the past, forgotten.

"Jesus is essentially a Lover. So tell Him you love Him."

— M.G., Durban, Republic of South Africa

◀ ▶

December 13

Although you have not seen Him,
you love Him;
and even though you do not see Him now,
you believe in Him and rejoice
with an indescribable and glorious joy.
— 1 Peter 1:8

John Cardinal O'Connor, the Archbishop of New York, once answered a question about his relationship with Jesus Christ. Here's what he told me:

"There is never a moment, no matter how depressed I am, no matter how discouraged, no matter how much pressure or tension I may be under, there is never a moment I do not feel the personal presence of Jesus Christ.

"It's a very, very personal relationship. Even when I'm tempted, Christ never goes away. And I don't know what I would do without that. I look at the Church as the Body of Christ, and I am immensely grateful to the Church."

◀ ▶

> *O Lord of hosts . . . look on the misery*
> *of your servant, and remember me.*
> — *1 Samuel 1:11*

Prayer is essentially giving yourself to God just as you are. Feelings can be helpful when they spur you on, but sometimes feelings like anger, loneliness or depression can get in the way. So don't fret about your feelings. True prayer is in the will to give yourself to God.

Remember the temptations of Jesus in the desert? And the desolation He felt during the agony in the Garden?

If that happens to you, just continue to give yourself to God as Jesus did. The important things to remember when you're lonely and in pain is that God is always with you and that you matter to Him.

Your pain. Your loneliness. These speak to God as loudly as your prayers. He is a compassionate and merciful God.

◄ ►

December 15

Rejoice before the Lord your God.
— Deuteronomy 16:11

Joy is a deep inner feeling that can fill our being, even in the midst of personal sufferings. It comes in part from realizing that we are here on earth for some definite purpose.

To find your God-given purpose in life involves an active and ultimately rewarding search. The priest-psychologist Ignace Lepp wrote, "If today there are so many joyless people around it is most probably because they have not found their right road or that for some reason or other they have not followed it."

Joy and peace seem to follow those who have persevered in their search for meaning. Even in sickness there is meaning if it is offered to God humbly for the salvation of many. Hold on to joy even in the midst of sorrow.

◀ ▶

I will satisfy the weary soul,
and every languishing soul I will replenish.
— *Jeremiah 31:25*

"Jesus Christ is the fulfillment of the prophesies of the Hebrew Bible. He is Lord, Savior, Son of God, Brother, Friend and Beloved.

"Jesus is everything. When I turn to Him I find peace, love, acceptance. He saves me from worries, anxieties and the pressures of life.

"With His light I see clearly. I see His beauty and love. I see truth. I see what is truly important. Jesus gives me perspective. He helps me focus on His love and on the art of living and sharing that love.

"When I spend time with Jesus, He shares Himself with me in a way that fills and satisfies me. Sometimes I search for something else to fill my emptiness or to calm my restlessness, but only He can quiet my restless soul.

"Only He gives me that peace which brings joy and sanity to my life. Today, Lord, give me Your peace."

— K.A.F., Carmel, IN

◀ ▶

You will forget your misery . . .
And your life will be brighter than the noonday.
— *Job 11:16,17*

The father of Martin Luther King, Jr., was also
a Baptist preacher from Birmingham, Alabama.
He managed to survive tragedy and continue his
work for the Lord with a cheerful heart. Not only
did he lose his son Martin to an assassin's bullet,
but his wife was murdered in an Atlanta church.
Imagine what he could have allowed himself to
become. And yet he followed the Lord's way of
forgiveness.

While speaking before a large audience years
later, he said, "Don't magnify what someone else
may be doing and minimize the wrongs on your
own part." He stressed the idea that we should
be reaching out to those in need. "The business
of the church," he insisted, "is to give everyone
a sense of belonging."

Martin Luther King, Sr., forgave the murderers
who took the lives of his son and wife. This
courageous act was possible only because his hope
was not in this world, his hope was in the Lord.

He believed in the coming of the Kingdom,
where every tear will be wiped away and every broken fence will be mended.

◄ ►

December 18

*On the twenty-fifth day of the ... month Chislev
(they) offered sacrifice ... on the new altar ...
All the people ... worshipped and blessed Heaven
... (and) celebrated the dedication of the altar
for eight days.*
— 1 Maccabees 4:52,53,55,56

Jesus observed the feast of Hanukkah.

The Hanukkah candles commemorate the eternal bridge of light which reaches from Creation itself to the radiant spirit of free men and women.

It is in this spirit that the Jewish Festival of Hanukkah — the Festival of Light — is celebrated.

On the Hanukkah menorah or candlestick, there is a ninth candle, the never-extinguished servant candle, that is used to light the other eight candles.

Like the ever-burning servant candle, you too burn brightest steadiest when you serve.

For us, Jesus is the Light of the world, the Suffering servant who comes not to condemn but to serve and to save.

◀ ▶

This is love,
that we walk according to His commandments . . .
you have heard it from the beginning
. . . walk in (love).
— 2 John 6

Jesus comes to enable us to love one another.

When we forgive, or listen, or act with courtesy toward those closest to us, we're really saying, "I love you."

A loving home life makes itself felt beyond its own boundaries. People who feel loved radiate love.

Practice charity at home. In that way your Christmas will be a beautiful reflection of God's own love.

◄ ►

We have our hope set on the living God,
who is the Savior of all people.
— 1 Timothy 4:10

"I'm a farmer in northwest Iowa. I also do plenty of volunteer work for my community and home town parish.

"I don't lose hope. In time things always work out. I love Jesus. I personally know that He died for me.

"He has blessed me time and time again. I'm not worthy of such goodness. I have sinned more than I could even start to count and again I'm forgiven without any questions.

"So who is Jesus, you ask? I'll tell you who He is. Jesus is my savior. My refuge. My rock. My friend. My brother. Yes, I do know Jesus! Jesus Christ is Lord. He's King, God from God, Light from Light. A man in all ways but sin. A beautiful, compassionate man.

"Need I say more? In fact I've run out of words to say.

"Praise God! Praise Jesus! Praise and thank You, Holy Spirit!"

— D.W., Storm Lake, IA

◄ ►

> *Keep alert, stand firm in your faith,*
> *be courageous, be strong.*
> *— 1 Corinthians 16:13*

Although the impulse to do good is rooted deeply in the fact that we are children of God, it must be recognized that we are also the descendants of Adam.

As a result, each of us is a mixture of moral weakness and spiritual strength. As Christ Himself said, *The spirit indeed is willing, but the flesh is weak.* (Matthew 26:41)

Humans were weakened to a great extent by Original Sin. We are, however, conscious that we ought to do good. We are called to fulfill a noble mission in life, even when we fail to do it.

This sense of "oughtness" can be dulled or blunted by constant wrongdoing, but it can never be totally eliminated.

In recognition of this, the divine prodding persists through thick and thin to urge us to live up to our true nature as a child of God and as a co-worker with Christ in building up His Kingdom.

◀ ▶

December 22

> *Blessed are you among women,*
> *and blessed is the fruit of your womb.*
> *And why has . . . the mother of my Lord*
> *come to me?*
> *— Luke 1:42-43*

Just as Mary was the first Christ-bearer, or Christopher, so are we carriers of Christ in this world. A Christopher believes:

■ That I am a child of God.

■ That Jesus is Lord.

■ That I have a mission to be a Christ-bearer in all areas of my life.

■ That I can help most by being cheerful, enthusiastic, positive and constructive in my actions.

■ That practicing the "Golden Rule" is a vital way of being God's instrument of love.

■ That my language, dress and actions should always reflect good taste and high moral standards.

■ That I should take a stand for: moral decency; honesty and integrity; family unity; and the sacredness of human life from conception to natural death.

◀ ▶

December 23

God's foolishness is wiser than human wisdom,
and God's weakness is stronger than
human strength.
— 1 Corinthians 1:25

We are all familiar with the Christmas story:
the Child in the manger, the young mother, Mary,
and her husband, Joseph, who had sought shelter
in a stable; the shepherds; the three wise men who
followed an unusual and brilliant star and offered
the Child gold, frankincense and myrrh.

What the Gospel depicted is not the revelation
of a powerful king surrounded by a splendid
court. There were no such symbols of power
which the world might recognize and respect.

What is shown is an Infant, a weak and helpless
Infant in His mother's arms.

Christians are asked to look upon this Infant
and to believe that He is the Son of God, the very
image of God's splendor and to recognize Him
as the Lord of history — the Messiah, the Savior,
the Truth, the Way, the Life.

The Wisdom of God contradicts the wisdom
of the world.

◀ ▶

While they were there, the time came for her to deliver her Child. And she gave birth to her firstborn Son and wrapped Him in bands of cloth, and laid Him in a manger because there was no place for them in the inn.
— *Luke 2:6-7*

"Jesus is my Way of Life. He is my all. My role Model, His Living Word, has been my guide to life.

"When I feel rejected and life's events seem too much to handle and I say 'why me?' I think of Mary and Joseph who were turned away from the inn. Of Jesus born in a stable.

"I think of how the Holy Family had to flee to Egypt; how God watched over them and delivered them safely back home. And I know that this same Compassionate Father is watching over me, too.

"Jesus is my Physician, he heals my spiritual hurts and emotional hurts. He is my strength.

"He is my Provider. He cares for all my needs. He is also my Discipliner. If I want something that's not good for me, He denies my request, because he loves me so much."

— G.D'A., Boston, MA

◄ ►

> *God so loved the world that He gave*
> *His only Son, so that everyone*
> *who believes in Him may not perish*
> *but may have eternal life.*
> *— John 3:16*

Jesus is the gift of God's love. The New Testament is overflowing with the Good News about the Father's love for us, and Jesus helps us to realize His love in a personal way.

Do not let your feelings sabotage your knowledge of God's love. Live joyfully in the awareness that you are a carrier of divine love.

You are a part of the supernatural Love-Force that brings healing to the world. You are a part of God's redemptive plan, and He delights in sharing His creative action with you.

Divine Love abides in you. You enter this unspeakable mystery of God's love by virtue of your union with His beloved Son, Jesus Christ. Through Him you participate in God's own life, and become a co-worker with Christ in bringing God's love to the world.

God calls you by name to the fullness of life and joy today and every day of the year.

◀ ▶

December 26

> *Those who seek the Lord*
> *lack no good thing.*
> *— Psalm 34:10*

A Bible which Abraham Lincoln often used as President falls open easily to Psalm 34. There is even a smudge at verse four where the President apparently often rested his fingers and meditated.

The verse reads: *I sought the Lord, and He answered me and delivered me from all my fears.*

Jesus encouraged us to pray:

Ask, and it will be given you; search, and you will find; knock, and the door will be opened for you. (Matthew 7:7)

Your Father in heaven will give good things to those who ask Him! (Matthew 7:11) Talk to your heavenly Father heart to heart, person to person as Jesus did. Express your emotions. Your genuine feelings.

You will be heard.

You are loved.

◄ ►

December 27

Go therefore and make disciples
of all nations . . .
teaching them to obey everything
that I have commanded you.
— Matthew 28:19,20

When the song of the angels is stilled,
When the star in the sky is gone,
When the kings and princes have gone home,
When the shepherds are back with their flock,
Then the work of Christmas begins:
    To find the lost,
    To heal the broken,
    To feed the hungry,
    To release the prisoner,
    To rebuild the nations,
    To bring peace,
    To make music in the heart.

◀ ▶

December 28

(God) has spoken to us by a Son ...
through whom He also created the worlds.
He is the reflection of God's glory
and the exact imprint of God's very being.
— *Hebrews 1:2-3*

Through figures of speech, images in words, Jesus gave us glimpses into that Mystery which is God.

As an itinerant Rabbi He spoke of The Kingdom as mustard seeds, baker's yeast, a fishing net, a vineyard.

He described His Abba, the Father, as the woman in search of her lost coin, the gladsome father of the prodigal, the farmer sowing seed.

Finally, Jesus spoke of Himself as a shepherd, a hen, life-giving bread, the gate to the sheepfold, a way, light and life-giving water.

At this season when we celebrate God's Son becoming Mary's Baby Boy, open yourself yet again to the Mystery of God.

Contemplate a helpless Infant in a manger and be filled with awe at the love and glory of the Lord.

◄ ►

*We boast in our sufferings knowing that
suffering produces endurance, and endurance
produces character, and character produces
hope, and hope does not disappoint us because
God's love has been poured into our hearts.*
— *Romans 5:3-5*

Suffering is an unavoidable part of life. Sometimes we have no real choice about it.

But we always have have a choice about the way we will face suffering.

We can endure unavoidable suffering grudgingly and resentfully, or we can accept the inevitable and try to live our lives around it finding meaning and even happiness where we can. One can mumble and complain or one can decide to face the future with cheerful acquiescence.

None of us are really alone in our troubles. God's strength works in and through us. In our weakness we all have to learn to rely on the power of Almighty God.

So lift up your heart and have a new confidence. Let today be a day of gratitude and cheer. With God's help you can find the secret well of joy deep in your soul and rejoice.

◄ ►

December 30

Lead a life worthy of the calling
to which you have been called,
with all humility and gentleness and patience,
bearing with one another in love.
— Ephesians 4:1-2

Father,
sometimes the family gets me down.
Bills pile up.
Relatives and friends make demands
on my time and attention.
I try to keep first things first.
To create an atmosphere where Your
name is honored, Your word observed.
But I become tired.
A hard edge creeps into my voice.

Help me to sustain a climate in which I
can grow in Your love.
Help me to develop fully the talents
You have given me.
Help me do my part to make this a
better world. Help me to be another
Christ.

Amen.

◀ ▶

December 31

When you are offering your gift at the altar,
if you remember that your brother or sister
has something against you, leave your gift there
. . . and go; first be reconciled to your
brother or sister, and then
come and offer your gift.
— Matthew 5:23-24

At Grace United Methodist Church in Atlanta, worshippers annually celebrate the end of the old year and the beginning of the new one with what they call a "burning service."

Each member of the congregation brings to the altar a paper on which he or she has written failures and mistakes, plus changes to be made during the new year. The paper is dropped into a flaming urn.

One year, two men who had once been friends, but had quarreled over a business deal, stood side by side at the altar. After dropping their papers into the urn, they faced each other and shook hands.

Beloved and blessed Trinity, Father, Son and Holy Spirit, help us as this year ends and a new year begins, to forgive each other from the heart.

◄ ►

Also Available

If you have enjoyed this book and are not familiar with other Christopher offerings, here is a brief description.

● **NEWS NOTES.** Over 40 titles are kept in print on a variety of topics and may be obtained in quantity. Single copies of back and future issues are free on request.

● **ECOS CRISTOFOROS.** Spanish translations of popular issues of News Notes. These too can be obtained in quantity. Single copies are free on request.

● **VIDEOCASSETTES.** There are now more than 70 titles in our Videocassette Library. They range from wholesome entertainment to serious discussions on family life, contemporary social issues, spiritual growth and more.

● **APPOINTMENT CALENDAR and MONTHLY PLANNER.** The calendar is designed to hang on the wall or keep on a desk. It contains an inspirational message for each day of the year and space for daily reminders. The Monthly Planner is handy for pocket or purse.

Fulfillment brochures and additional information about The Christophers can be obtained by writing: THE CHRISTOPHERS, 12 East 48th St., New York, NY 10017.